My Zinc Bed

David Hare was born in Sussex in 1947. In 1970 his first play *Slag* was performed at the Hampstead Theatre Club. In 1993 three of his plays, *Racing Demon, Murmuring Judges* and *The Absence of War*, were presented together in repertory at the Olivier Theatre in London. Since 1983, nine of his best-known plays, including *Plenty, The Secret Rapture, Skylight, The Judas Kiss, Amy's View* and *Via Dolorosa,* have also been presented on Broadway.

DAVID HARE

My Zinc Bed

ff

faber and faber

First published in 2000
by Faber and Faber Limited
3 Queen Square London WC1N 3AU

Typeset by Country Setting, Kingsdown, Kent CT14 8ES
Printed in England by Mackays of Chatham plc, Chatham, Kent

A CIP record for this book
is available from the British Library

ISBN 0–571–20574–7

2 4 6 8 10 9 7 5 3 1

for Nicole, my love

My Zinc Bed was first presented at the Royal Court Theatre, London, on 14 September 2000. The cast was as follows:

Paul Peplow Steven Mackintosh
Victor Quinn Tom Wilkinson
Elsa Quinn Julia Ormond

Director David Hare
Designer Vicki Mortimer
Lighting Designer Rick Fisher

Characters

Paul Peplow
Elsa Quinn
Victor Quinn

MY ZINC BED

There is no Shakespeare; there is no Beethoven;
certainly and emphatically there is no God;
we are the words; we are the music;
we are the thing itself.

Virginia Woolf

Act One

ONE

*The stage is a black void. It is important that its exact
shape and size can only be sensed. Paul Peplow stands
before us, alone. He's an attractive man, in his early
thirties, thin, saturnine, tousled, as if he has just woken
up. He wears an untidy linen suit and a tie, and his
manner is self-deprecating.*

Paul Joseph Conrad says that inside every heart there
burns a desire to set down once and for all a true record
of what has happened. For myself, nothing that has
happened, nothing that can happen, compares with the
passage of a single summer, from May to September, the
cyber-summer when I first met Elsa Quinn.

TWO

*Victor Quinn has appeared along a corridor of light and
is advancing towards Paul, already talking. He is in his
early fifties, anonymous, thickly built. His background is
hard to place, for he has lost his native Northern accent.
He has the air of a man whose power is held always in
reserve. He wears an expensive suit, but no tie. It is not
yet clear where we are, but, wherever, it is plainly
Victor's home turf and Paul is the guest. The space
around them remains undefined.*

Victor 'Many are the stories with interesting beginnings,
but harder to find are the stories which end well.'

He stops short of Paul, not yet shaking his hand.

Paul I'm sorry?

Victor Surely you can't have forgotten.

Paul Oh, I see.

Victor Your own words.

Paul Yes.

Victor Though maybe you write so many you lose track. (*He smiles and shakes Paul's hand.*) Victor Quinn.

Paul Paul Peplow.

Victor Of course.

Victor gestures towards a chair, leaving Paul free to sit or stand as he chooses.

'End well' in which sense? A story which ends well, meaning 'well', meaning happily for its subject, or 'well', meaning in a way which satisfies the reader? Or did you intend both? Is the ambiguity deliberate?

Paul Both, I think. It was just a book review.

Victor looks at him a moment.

Victor I can't believe that's what you really feel.

Paul waits, not willing to show his discomfiture.

Drink?

Paul No thank you.

Victor Of course. Wrong of me to ask. (*He flashes a smile at Paul.*) Well. As you know, I don't often agree to be interviewed.

Paul It's kind of you.

Victor Not at all.

4

Paul Why are you normally so reclusive?

Victor Have we started?

Paul has reached into his pocket and got out a notebook.

Ah. The book's coming out.

Paul Please.

Victor How can you call me a recluse? I live in the centre of London.

Paul But you don't give interviews.

Victor I'm not an exhibitionist, no. I'm a simple man. My question is always 'To what end?' To what end would I tell people, say, my favourite restaurant? My favourite tailor? That the world should beat a path to the restaurant? That I should have to wait longer for my suit?

Paul Do you have a tailor?

Victor No. I buy off-the-peg.

Paul makes a note.

If you'd like something to eat.

Paul No thank you. And how did you know I would refuse a drink?

Victor Ah.

Paul Did someone tell you?

Victor smiles, pleased with this question.

Victor I believe you belong to what cooks on television call the vulnerable groups.

Paul I've never heard that expression.

Victor 'Remember: don't put brandy in this pudding, it endangers the vulnerable groups.' You don't need to say more. I know about these things. 'Hello my name is Victor. I'm an alcoholic.' You see. I've followed the course myself.

Paul It's not really a course.

Victor No. A course implies an end . . .

Paul Yes.

Victor And in this case there is no end. (*He looks at Paul thoughtfully.*) I've studied the meetings. At the time I was trying to understand the techniques.

Paul What techniques exactly?

Victor Well, Paul, we can talk about anything you like. But for this particular subject, you first have to concede the accuracy of my intelligence. (*He waits for Paul.*) I'm sorry.

Paul No.

Victor If you're reluctant.

Paul hesitates a moment.

Paul I go to the meetings, yes.

Victor Yes, that's what I thought.

Paul I have no idea how you know. To be honest I'm surprised you've heard of me at all.

Victor England is a series of clubs. No club more celebrated, no club more socially advantageous than yours. Under the guise of admitting their fallibility, people meet in fact to advance their own cause.

Paul You obviously didn't go very often.

Victor No. (*Victor gestures at Paul to encourage him to speak.*) You say. You say what you think these meetings are.

Paul A means . . . one means of people helping one another.

Victor looks at Paul for a moment in a way which makes it clear that Victor thinks him naive.

I suppose we should start by discussing FLOTILLA.

Victor Go ahead.

Paul Its recent move to the stock market.

Victor A transparent success. What's your question?

Paul Whether you did it for the money.

For the first time Victor looks impatient.

Victor Now perhaps you understand my distrust. What do I answer? 'I did it for the money.' People will think I'm greedy. 'I didn't do it for the money.' Then they'll say I'm unworldly. More likely, I'm lying. I'm a hypocrite. Paul, you of all people understand: the modern newspaper interview is a form as rigid and contrived as the eighteenth-century gavotte.

Paul Shall I just put: he refused to answer?

Victor Meaning: he's a prick.

They both smile.

He consented to an interview, then he wouldn't answer the questions!

Paul Why 'of all people'? Why did you say 'me of all people'?

Victor A poet.

Paul Ah.

Victor I read poetry. I read yours.

Love was the search, the wheel, the line,
The open road and the steep incline;
Things speeding by, the final turn in view,
Next: something disastrous, overwhelming, new.

I hardly believe you would now be paddling in journalism
if it weren't purely for the money.

Paul No.

Victor You'll drink to that.

Paul Yes. So to speak. (*Paul smiles, amused by Victor's
manner.*)

Victor I liked the idea, I promise you.

Paul Of this interview?

Victor No. Of the meetings. I thought the meetings
amusing.

Paul Amusing? Obviously you aren't alcoholic.

Victor I'm not.

Paul The meetings are a discipline.

Victor Of course. They wouldn't be addictive if they
weren't.

Paul now understands Victor's point.

Paul Oh I see . . .

Victor All cults make similar demands.

Paul I think it's childish, people calling AA a cult. It's
ignorant. I tell you what: I actually believe it's quite
dangerous.

Victor Do you? I'd have thought it's a classic cult.

Paul Why?

Victor The chairs, the coffee, the soul-searching . . .
(*Victor hastens to explain.*) Believe me, I'm not denying
its usefulness.

Paul You couldn't.

Victor It is the means by which many people survive. Or
they believe it is.

Paul It saved my life.

There is a short silence.

I was found on the M4, dodging the traffic. And naked,
in the middle of the night.

Victor Huh.

Paul I don't need to question the value of AA.

Victor is completely still.

Victor What brought you there? What brought you to
the motorway so late at night?

Paul does not answer.

It's none of my business. You're right. Presumably you
believe that one drink will take you on the road to hell?

Paul I do believe that, yes.

Victor It's what they teach you.

Paul It's also what I believe.

Victor It isn't true, you know.

Paul Isn't it?

Victor Of course not. The cult makes rules. It demands
obedience. The cult has invented the slogan: One Drink,
One Drunk. But it isn't actually true. If you had cured

9

your own addiction, in the privacy of your own home, then you could perfectly well drink socially again.

Paul I'm not going to take that risk.

Victor You can't take that risk, you mean?

Again, Paul says nothing.

'Candy is dandy but liquor is quicker.' Do they still say that?

Paul They do. (*Paul watches Victor mistrustfully.*)

Victor I'm making you uncomfortable.

Paul Is this relevant?

Victor To what? I'm making you nervous, I see.

Paul No, I'm not nervous. I'm meant to do an interview, that's all. That's what I'm doing here. You make me seem boring. And obsessive. 'I've got an interview to do.' I sound like a bore.

Victor Well, let's be fair. Do the interview, I get nothing out of this meeting. Tell me about alcoholism, I may profit as well.

Paul looks a moment, resolving to be straight with him.

Paul There's nothing to say.

Victor Nothing?

Paul I have no theories. Theories don't interest me.

Victor No?

Paul I have one aim in life . . .

Victor Just one?

Paul My aim is to get to bed sober tonight. That's

my aim. And I have found pragmatically – excuse me, I know a little about this – that the only means of achieving it is through attendance at AA. It's the only method which works.

He's finished. Victor smiles.

Victor Have you thought . . . have you considered what it would mean to be cured?

Paul Of course. Naturally.

Victor Are you sure?

Paul I think of little else.

Victor But that's my point. If you can't drink at all – ever – then by definition you're not cured.

Paul What's your idea of cured?

Victor 'Thank you. I'll just have the one. Just the one for me. Thank you.' (*Victor smiles, pleased with his own answer.*) You should think about it, Paul. Consider. It's only groups which demand total abstinence. Why? Because their intention is not to stop you drinking. That is only a side-aim. Their principal aim is to retain you as a member of the group.

Paul It's a familiar argument. It's also nonsense.

Victor Really? I'm interested. Tell me why.

There is a moment's pause before Paul decides to take the plunge.

Paul Look, if you really want to know . . .

Victor I do.

Paul Of course I went into AA kicking and screaming.

Victor Ah.

Paul Everyone does. What I'm saying is: at the end of a very long story. Which I am not going to tell you. Believe me, I had a thousand reservations . . .

Victor But presumably you'd bottomed . . .

Paul Yes.

Victor That's the phrase they use.

Paul I bottomed.

Victor The M4.

Paul Not just the M4. Not just that one night, believe me.

Victor Other nights?

Paul looks at him a moment.

Paul You wake up in the morning and you've fallen down three flights of stairs. But even so. Even then. I was still reluctant. I clung to the thought: I'm not the sort of person who sits in a circle stripping himself bare.

Victor I'm sure. A poet.

Paul Even when I was young, at college, in the student common room, come that dreaded moment, come eleven, come twelve, people have been drinking – beer in those days, of course – and they begin to spill. How unhappy they are. How pointless life is.

Victor Yes.

Paul You can imagine. I was out of that room like a shot.

Victor Somehow I see you alone with a girl come midnight.

Paul Whatever. I was not in the common room, telling all and sundry my innermost thoughts. (*Paul is suddenly*

12

insistent.) However. You go to the meetings because you have to. Because it's your last chance. Your only chance. And it doesn't matter who you think you once were, what sense of yourself you once had, that identity you were once convinced was *you* – you left that person behind in the gutter with his pride and his empty bottle and his, 'Oh I'd never join a cult . . . ' (*He looks at Victor, using his word.*) If we were alone on this earth then what would it matter? Who cares? You work that one out pretty quickly. Oh sure, everyone has the right to destroy their own life. But to destroy the lives of others?

Victor Ah yes. 'Others.' (*Victor has stopped, thoughtful.*)

Paul You're right. I was frightened of AA. Yes. Why do you think I was frightened?

Victor I'd have thought it was obvious.

Paul Not at all. I was frightened because in my heart I knew it would work.

Victor I see.

Paul Yes.

Victor Because it works?

Paul That's why. I no sooner walked into the room than I intuited: Oh my God, this is going to work. And when the fifteen-year-old daughter of a Scottish plumber calls you in the middle of the night to ask if you can come and help her father who has passed out in the toilet, then – forgive me – you don't think, 'Oh yes, this is really helping my career.' If you want personal advancement, stay in the pub. (*Paul shakes his head.*) My resistance now seems ridiculous.

Victor Why?

Paul 'I'm not the sort of person who does this,' you say. But what sort of person are you by that stage? What have you become? A worthless drunk.

Victor Yes. It's that word 'worthless' I have trouble with.

Paul looks at him a moment, distressed.

Paul I'm sorry. Plainly I shouldn't have come here.

Victor No. I apologise.

Paul I didn't come to talk about this stuff. (*Paul struggles painfully through what he says next.*) I'll be honest. I have only recently, with great difficulty, begun once more to write for the papers because – again – we seem to be talking about me – I have to avoid stress. (*Then Paul turns to Victor and laughs.*) I'm broke. Yeah. I'm completely broke. I don't have a fucking penny in the world. I can't get a bank account. The editor pays me in cash.

Victor Where do you live?

Paul Camberwell.

Victor shrugs to say that isn't so bad.

Paul Stretching the charity of a last remaining friend. You?

Victor Regent's Park.

Paul Good. Well, that's something solid for the article.

Paul's sudden unsteadiness has brought them close. Victor speaks quietly, opening up for the first time.

Victor I was a communist.

Paul Yes.

Victor waits.

What are you saying? Is that how your interest in cults came about?

Victor Sort of. Apparently the newspapers have taken to calling me a one-time Marxist. They can't bring themselves to use the proper word. I'm most insistent. I wasn't a Marxist. I was a communist. I use the full shocker.

Paul All or nothing, eh?

Victor That sort of thing.

Paul And you mean it was a cult? There were rules?

Victor Conditions of membership, yes. All clubs have membership rules or they aren't clubs.

Paul England, you were saying . . .

Victor Yes. A series of clubs. The English love clubs. Not of course for the pleasure of allowing people in . . .

Paul No.

Victor Oh no! The far headier delight of keeping people out! They love that! English communists, we were a select little band. A snotty little group we were.

Paul And presumably the moment came when you began to see club rules as arbitrary . . .

Victor It took a long time. For a long time, I subscribed.

Paul It's a familiar progress, isn't it, from student politics? Communist to entrepreneur?

Victor I still believe in history. A way of looking at things historically. You never lose that. The computer comes along. It's the next thing.

Paul But they took years to develop.

Victor For years you walked past them. Everyone did.

They were just whopping great dinner plates spinning in glass-panelled rooms. Then suddenly – whoosh. Of themselves uninteresting. But you spot the moment. The fortunes were made very quickly, as you probably know. (*Victor shrugs.*) Not that I claim any credit.

Paul You could equally well have been wrong.

Victor Exactly.

Paul What were you doing before?

Victor Importing virgin olive oil. Stupid, I agree. I mistook changes in life-style for historical shifts. That's what I mean. I'm as vulnerable to bullshit as everyone else.

They are getting on well now. Paul is taking notes, more relaxed now.

When I left the Party I was penniless. Like you. I was a tour guide for a while.

Paul On top of a double-decker?

Victor Correct. I specialised in misleading information. I used to love pointing out the place where General Eisenhower, to thank the British people for their heroic war effort, had built a life-size statue of Mickey Mouse. The whole bus craned their necks to see.

Paul That's funny.

Victor I always said 'life-size'. I loved saying 'life-size'. 'We are now passing the spot where Lord Nelson first made love to Lady Hamilton . . . ' I usually chose the Elephant and Castle.

Paul What are you saying?

Victor They saw it, you see. They saw the statue.

Paul People are gullible?

Victor No. They're romantic. They see the statue when it isn't there. (*Victor smiles, pleased at the thought. He too is becoming less guarded.*) Capitalists make me laugh because they understand nothing. They talk about strategy and markets as if they were in control.

Paul And aren't they?

Victor They use soothing devices like big cars and hotels and servants. They use luxury as a sort of massage to persuade themselves they've acted brilliantly, that their actions have been brilliant . . .

Paul Whereas in fact?

Victor shrugs.

Victor They've worked hard and had a bit of luck.

Paul Don't you use big cars?

Victor Never. Or only for the children, anyway.

Paul How many children do you have?

Victor There's an advantage to seeing things historically. It makes you less self-important. (*Victor pauses, wanting to lay down a principle.*) Communism is night-class. It's where you learn. Who is doing what to whom? If you don't believe that the rich spend their time on this earth effectively fucking over the poor, then I don't see how you make any sense of what goes on in the world at all.

Paul smiles, risking his neck a little.

Paul But, forgive me, nobody could mistake your wealth.

Victor No?

Paul I don't think so. To look at you, it's clear.

Victor Is it? I'm rather insulted.

Paul You make certain assumptions. If you don't mind my saying.

Victor (*watchful*) Say more.

Paul Well, I've noticed you use certain techniques. Which, rightly or wrongly, I associate with the rich. Or at least with the powerful.

Victor What techniques are those?

Paul What I mean is: you'd read my poetry.

Victor Well?

Paul Is it a manner? Is it a game? You read my poetry before the meeting. You put yourself instantly at an advantage. 'I know who you are. I've read *This Too Shall Pass.*'

Victor Yes. I see. You think that's specifically a technique of the rich?

Paul And, what's more, learning a whole verse.

Victor 'Love was the search, the wheel, the line . . . '

Paul A line maybe, but a whole verse!

Victor Too much?

Paul If the purpose was to unsettle me, then I'm afraid you've succeeded. I've been uncomfortable ever since you arrived.

Victor Forgive me, but I think you would have been uncomfortable however I approached you.

> *Paul blushes, caught off-guard. He reaches for his notebook in confusion.*

Paul We'd better go on.

Victor I'm sorry. I went too far.

Paul I'm fine.

Victor I do that. Are you all right?

Paul I'm fine. (*He isn't. He takes a second to recover.*)
When did you leave the Party?

Victor 1975.

Paul And do you miss it?

Victor Let's say, it's like New Zealand. I'm glad it's there
but I have no wish to visit.

Paul Put it another way: do you regret its decline?

*Paul is not letting go. Victor looks at him, a little
wistful.*

Victor It's the world that's changed, not me. Or changed
more than me.

Paul In what way?

Victor Something has happened which I don't pretend
to understand. We are now told that managing things is
a technical skill. What you manage is irrelevant. All
businesses are essentially the same.

Paul Is that what you believe yourself?

Victor That's what they tell us. Politicians boast of being
plumbers, not architects. The word 'ideological' is never
now mentioned.

Paul Except with the word 'baggage'.

Victor That's right. (*Victor thinks about it a moment.*)
Now we solve problems. Everything is a problem, and
we solve it. We say, what is the problem? We define it.
Nothing is decided in advance, because nothing is believed
in advance. It's as simple as that. That's how we proceed.
That's how we get things done. The containable life.

(*Victor stares at Paul a moment.*) You know what I'm saying?

Paul I do.

Victor You could say the whole world's in AA.

Paul is quiet, speaking after a moment.

Paul Can I ask you something else?

Victor Please.

Paul It's nothing to do with business.

Victor Please.

Paul What's your interest in the meetings?

Victor looks momentarily evasive.

Victor I had a friend who quit.

Paul Quit alcohol?

Victor No. Quit AA. Much harder. (*Victor is cautious.*) It was when you used the word 'worthless'. I reacted. Sorry. Now it's my turn to be reluctant, I think.

Paul Why?

Victor Because my friend came home one evening . . .

Paul Came home? To your home, you mean?

Victor I have no right to say this.

Paul You're betraying a confidence?

Victor Not at all. My friend would happily tell you herself. She tells anyone who's interested.

Paul Well then?

Victor My scruples are not towards her but towards you.

Paul Me? (*Paul frowns, disbelieving.*) I'm in a bad way, I know. Even crossing the Thames has become an undertaking. It's true. I go out very little. I listen to music at home. But I'm strong enough to cope with ideas.

Victor Good, then.

Paul I'm not frightened of ideas.

Victor looks at him, as if fearing for him, then proceeds cautiously.

Victor I remember very clearly. My friend came back from a meeting. She had seen things for a moment with an outsider's eye. She had become convinced that the purpose of the cult was to reinforce her feelings of worthlessness, not to try and assuage them.

Paul What made her feel that?

Victor She never went back. (*Victor sits back, as if having said the final word.*)

Paul Surely she knew she would have to confront her illness?

Victor Confront it by all means, but then move on.

Paul Do you think an addict can ever move on?

Victor Ah well.

Paul Truly?

Victor You're right. This was at the heart of the issue.

Paul It is. It is at the heart.

Victor You may say that she regarded her escape from AA as a far greater triumph than her escape from addiction. (*Victor nods.*) I asked you earlier what class you belonged to. You didn't answer. No need. You belong to the confessional class. The class most people belong to nowadays.

Paul That's the old Marxist speaking.

Victor My friend felt they were replacing her dependency on drugs with a dependency on coffee and confession, on what you would call the dreaded circle of chairs. They were sustaining her – how do I put this? – in a sort of suspended anxiety. They were instilling what would become a permanent fear of the great crash round the corner. (*Victor shrugs.*) She came to feel no crash could be as terrible as the fear of that crash. In order to preserve that fear and to magnify it, they were forbidding her self-respect.

Paul In that case I don't believe she was alcoholic.

Victor No?

Paul An alcoholic has no self-respect.

> *Victor looks at Paul a moment. Then he speaks, silvery.*

Victor I gave her a gin and tonic. She drank it. And we then played Scrabble all evening.

> *Victor looks deeply pleased at this, but Paul is not buying it.*

Paul I don't believe she was addictive in the first place.

Victor Believe what you like.

Paul I don't believe it.

> *Victor is now looking at him very hard.*

Victor Paul, it seems to me you have a problem of self-esteem.

Paul How so? In what way, specifically?

Victor Why did I agree to meet you?

Paul I have no idea.

Victor Think about it. It would hardly be with the aim of wishing to appear in your paper.

Paul No.

Victor It's not a paper for which one volunteers. (*Victor looks at him sardonically.*) You accuse me of mugging up your poetry with the purpose of flattering you.

Paul It's not quite what I said.

Victor Does it not occur to you – does it really not occur to you? – that you insult yourself with this suggestion more than you insult me?

Paul I don't understand.

Victor Do I have to spell it out?

He waits a moment, looking at Paul, who still doesn't get it.

Your poetry is the reason I have long wanted to meet you.

Paul Oh. Oh, I see.

Paul is taken aback. He searches for a reply, but Victor is ahead of him.

Victor What did you like to drink?

Paul I'm sorry?

Victor What was your favourite drink?

Paul Mine?

Victor Yes.

Paul A fatal weakness for Manhattans.

Victor I would never have guessed. Fiddling about with cherries, you think that's time well spent?

Paul And you?

Victor Oh. I like a Martini.

Paul As well spent as fiddling about with olives.

Victor Hmm. (*Victor is considering Paul thoughtfully.*) And if I offered you one now . . .

   Paul just looks at him.

That's it, isn't it? If you were cured, you would be cured of the desire. And who wants to be cured of desire? (*Victor decides suddenly to wind up the meeting.*) It's been a great pleasure to meet you. I have given up reading the newspapers, but my impression is that the modern practice is for the journalist to write the story before the encounter. What I am saying is: write what you like. Your poetry has a flair for the dramatic. I trust that flair. Invent my character, by all means. I shall stand by whatever opinions you ascribe to me. I shall be your invention.

Paul Thank you.

Victor Consider yourself liberated from the facts. (*He shakes Paul's hand.*) I'd very much like it if we could meet again.

Paul Yes. I'd like that too.

   Victor turns and goes.

You didn't tell me. How's your friend doing?

Victor Oh. She's doing fine.

THREE

Victor has gone. Paul turns from the scene and speaks directly towards us. Behind him, the feeling of the stage changes to suggest the new location.

24

Paul As job interviews go, it was one of the more peculiar. No piece ever appeared. I told the editor that my subject had been a no-show. He said it was typical of the man's notorious arrogance not even to turn up. I started working for Victor the following week.

FOUR

Elsa Quinn is sitting on top of Paul's desk, her feet on a chair below her. Once more, the surrounding area is undefined, but it is evening, and this time we are in a large place of work. There is a feeling of modern technology. Overhead lights stretch away into the distance. Elsa is in her early thirties. She is wearing a short dark skirt and a white shirt. She is Danish by birth, but, again, next to nothing of her accent remains. At this moment, she has a pleasant air of amusement, as if someone has just told her a joke. Paul is instantly at ease with her in a way he can never be with Victor.

Elsa And so what was she like?

Paul Who?

Elsa This woman. This woman who drove you nuts.

Paul You'd have to meet her for yourself to decide.

Elsa Why?

Paul *Why?* Because why do you think? Why do you think, for goodness' sake? Because from me you will get a partial account.

Elsa Why?

Paul Because . . . Oh just, *because*! Why do you think?

Elsa She really got to you?

Paul has no need to answer. They smile together.

Paul And also she wanted to be an actress, which was also not easy. Because I had to watch television – and . . .

Elsa That's not such a hardship.

Paul I don't know . . . look at her in helmets and things.

Elsa Viking helmets?

Paul No. Police helmets. Obviously.

Elsa It's not obvious.

Paul It's what actors have to do. Or the ones she knew. They play police all the time. Or doctors. They play very few Vikings. She was a doctor for a bit in a series where they went to the cupboards at the ends of the wards and made love.

Elsa frowns.

Young doctors, you know, working thirty-five-hour shifts and fucking each other in the middle of the night.

Elsa I don't think I saw that one.

Paul They did it in the police series, too. Same idea. We're So Tired All We Can Do Is. Under-funding as eroticism, that sort of thing.

Elsa You had to watch your girlfriend with other people?

Paul Simulating, yes.

Elsa How was that?

Paul Not bad, actually. Quite fun, actually, in a kind of way. (*Paul laughs.*) I always think I should have minded it more.

Elsa Yes. I think it must be interesting.

Paul Yes.

There is a long silence. Elsa re-crosses her legs. Paul just sits, thinking.

I minded it more when she did it in real life.

Elsa looks at him a moment. It's a decisive confidence on his part.

Elsa Is that why it ended?

Paul Oh.

Elsa It is over?

Paul Oh yes. Long over. (*Paul thinks, then casually springs back to life.*) And apart from anything there's the ridiculous incongruity.

Elsa Like?

Paul Explaining to a friend, 'Oh I'm crazy about this woman, she's so extraordinary, I'm going out of my mind.' They say, 'Do you mean the dark one?' I say, 'No, the dark one plays the radiotherapist.' 'Oh the blonde,' they say. 'It's the blonde you want to kill yourself for.'

Elsa Crazy.

Paul It seems so arbitrary.

Elsa Yes.

Paul It's this disparity. Because she was this face on television so everyone thought they knew her. But in fact only I knew her.

Elsa Only you?

Paul stops, the pain of it fresh.

Paul Well, me and the dozen others. The dirty dozen, as I came to think of them.

Elsa watches, not moving.

Elsa Why did you say, 'She wanted to be an actress'?

Paul Did I?

Elsa You said, 'She wanted to be an actress.'

Paul Oh yes.

Elsa But she was an actress.

Paul That's what I'm saying. In the world's eyes. To me, she was something else.

Elsa What was her name?

Paul ignores the question. He turns to Elsa.

Paul What about you?

Elsa Oh . . .

Paul Any such figure in your life? Why are we talking about this?

Elsa Because I asked you.

Paul You talk to me as if I were seventeen.

Elsa Do I?

Paul In fact we're probably both the same age.

Elsa Yes. Probably. (*Elsa smiles.*) It's often more interesting . . . don't you think . . .?

Paul In what way?

Elsa Talking to people you don't know?

Paul Maybe. I don't live that kind of life any more.

Elsa What? What life?

Paul Oh you know. Girls. Bars.

28

Elsa Well, nor do I.

Paul Look at me, for goodness' sake! (*Paul gestures round the empty space.*) I stay behind in the office. What am I doing here? The last man to leave!

Elsa I can see. I'm impressed.

Paul Because girls go with bars in my mind and bars are long since forbidden. Sitting up. Talking. Pat your pcokects. 'Oh God, I've forgotten my key.' I don't do it any more.

Elsa Bars frighten you?

Paul smiles at the understatement.

Paul No. Everything frightens me.

They share the absurdity and the moment unlocks him.

Oh look, well what happens is . . . for goodness' sake you know about this . . .

Elsa Do I?

Paul You're focused on one thing, aren't you?

Elsa You tell me.

Paul Your recovery. Isn't that right?

Elsa I'm sure.

Paul You want to recover. That's all you want. Or you think it's all you want. (*Paul checks with Elsa.*) And the other person . . . well, the other person has got tired of clearing up . . . you can't blame them, it's fair enough, they're just tired of tidying up after . . .

Elsa Well, yes.

Paul You know about this?

Elsa gives nothing away.

Elsa Go on.

Paul Every night you're sick. You're reeling. Whatever. You're in agony.

Elsa The guilt!

Paul Exactly.

Elsa You're drinking again!

Paul And the other person says, she says, 'I don't want to play nurse. I refuse to play nurse. I won't do it.' Especially when they play nurse on the television already.

Elsa And doctor. And policewoman.

Paul Exactly. (*Paul begins to nod, gaining momentum.*) So then after a while you start to think, OK, this isn't too bad, I'm beginning to clean up, I'm sober – hey, this is really much better.

Elsa One day at a time.

Paul Precisely. As you say. You think: at last. I deserve a fucking break.

Elsa You do deserve a break. It's true.

Paul I've been to fifty thousand fucking meetings. And I deserve a break.

Elsa And? Instead?

Paul looks at her, deciding once more how far to go.

Instead?

Paul Instead – like the trick of an actress to be – I don't know – not to play roles exactly, no she doesn't do that, Clem didn't do that – but to slither about, to slide all the time. And you long for someone who is constant . . .

30

Elsa Yes.

Paul You have no right to ask, God knows you have no rights – you're a snake, you know that, you're lower than a snake – but you do long for someone who does not slither about. (*Paul looks up to make sure she understands.*)

Elsa Yes.

Paul Then one day she turns to you, your girlfriend turns to you, she informs you that she is an honest person, she is an unusual human being . . .

Elsa Oh yes?

Paul . . . because she cannot live in an atmosphere of lies, she cannot bear dishonesty. 'Sorry,' she says, but 'that's my character' – so she must tell you she's been meeting other people, other people who are, as it were, *not you*, the reason being, Clem says, that you were a drunk and so what was she meant to do?

Elsa Do you believe her?

Paul Believe her how? What, believe she slept with them?

Elsa No, believe her reasons.

Paul She slept with a dozen other men. A dozen. Finally, what the hell do her reasons matter?

For the first time Paul lets his feelings show. Elsa watches from the desktop, still giving nothing away.

Elsa They matter.

Paul And then, well then, when you've been clean for a week or two she turns round – you are struggling to hold on, you are struggling to maintain the relationship – she looks at you and she says: you know what she says?

Elsa I think I can guess.

Paul She says . . .

Elsa Tell me.

Paul You're warming up the dinner from Marks and Spencers. You've turned on the television. You're pouring the Coca-Cola. She says, 'Do you know something, Paul? Since you've tried to clean up you've got kind of *boring*. Have you noticed? You were so much more interesting when you were drunk.'

Elsa Yes.

Paul shakes his head at the scale of the injustice.

And were you?

Paul Early on she said, 'No commitments.' Later I said, 'I agreed, no commitments. But somehow when you said no commitments, forgive me, I did not foresee the number twelve.'

Elsa Twelve? Are you sure she said twelve?

Paul Somehow . . . trust me . . . the figure has lodged in my mind.

Elsa acknowledges his point.

Anyway then the plan is, the project is: you are to return to the meetings . . . 'Hello. My name is Paul. I'm an alcoholic.'

Elsa And go through the scene . . .

Paul Yes . . .

Elsa Discuss the *details* of the scene . . .

Paul Exactly.

Elsa Go into . . .

Paul Yes.

Elsa . . . her duodecimal behaviour . . .

Paul looks despairingly at her.

Paul Mind you, I'm not saying – let's be clear, AA is my sole hope, my sole source of hope . . .

Elsa Is it?

Paul For sure. I should be there now.

Elsa 'Should'? 'Should'?

Paul But you'll understand if occasionally I say, 'I can't get to the meeting, I couldn't get to the meeting, I was held up at FLOTILLA, I ran into the boss's wife . . .'

Elsa I'm glad you did. I'm really glad.

There is a moment suspended between them. Then Elsa turns away, a little distant now as she speaks.

Victor says, what will it matter when we're dead?

Paul I'm sorry?

Elsa No, it's something he says.

Paul Goodness.

Elsa That's all. 'It matters today. It matters tomorrow. But what will it matter when we're dead?' He has that advantage, you see.

Paul Seeing it all as history?

Elsa Yes. Plus he's older than us.

They share the joke. Elsa gestures at the surrounding technology.

Computers are crap because they're just beginning. So they have to be crap. How can they not be crap? They've just started. They will inevitably be crap for the next twenty years. Then they'll get good. It doesn't bother him.

Paul What does bother him?

She considers Paul for a moment.

Elsa People don't want to know me. They want to know my husband. Or rather they want to know me because that way they get to meet my husband.

Paul Does that upset you?

Elsa Not at all. It amuses me.

Paul Why?

Elsa I've a life of my own. And let's face it, he's a fascinating man. Why should people not want to meet him?

Paul Indeed. Have you been together long?

Elsa The first time he saw me, he always claims I was wearing a T-shirt which said, 'They've put a man on the moon. Why can't they put the rest of them there?' He says the challenge was irresistible.

Paul It would be.

Elsa hesitates a moment.

Elsa When he met me, I was a drunk.

There is a silence. They look at each other, straight in the eye, a deep bond between them. In the distance, the bell of a City church chimes. Then Paul looks away.

Paul The most interesting thing about computers . . .

Elsa Yes?

Paul . . . I have observed, is just how often they go down on you.

Elsa Really?

Paul Do you find that?

Elsa To be honest I know very little about them.

Paul It's so odd. A universally popular piece of technology whose primary characteristic is its chronic unreliability. The bugger'll go down as soon as look at you. Breathe on the bugger, it goes down.

Elsa Victor says that's why people like them. The possibility they can lose everything in a flash. Victor says what he's selling is risk.

Paul Well he's right.

Elsa The blue screen of death!

> *Elsa flicks back her hair. Again, Paul looks away because he is enjoying her too much.*

Paul I've discovered a web-site. Did Victor tell you this?

Elsa No.

Paul I'm surprised.

Elsa He said nothing.

Paul It's for those customers who wish to share their experiences of using FLOTILLA software.

Elsa Bitter, are they?

Paul It's called www.fuckvictorquinn.com. It had 50,000 hits in one week.

Elsa I would guess he was thrilled.

Paul All he said was, 'It adds to my mystique.'

Elsa That's Victor.

Paul Victor said, 'They resent me because I give them possibility. Possibility unsettles them because it is not perfection.'

Elsa smiles at how Victor-like this sounds.

Was he always oracular?

Elsa Since I met him.

Paul When he's alone? Having supper, for instance? Is it like visiting Delphi?

Elsa Not exactly. No. What are you asking?

Paul Well . . .

Elsa He does unbend.

Paul Ah.

Elsa He's a boy from Manchester who got taken up by Lancashire communists at the age of fifteen.

Paul So?

Elsa Whatever shell he has, he's acquired.

Paul But underneath?

Elsa The style – declamatory, expository – he got it from Marx, he says. And the *Manchester Evening News*. Which he also read at a formative age.

Paul Yes.

Elsa Plus you do need a brain.

There is a silence. Elsa is thinking.

He isn't confusing. That's the point. I like the way you know where you are.

Silently, overhead squares of light begin to go out

36

around them in irregular rhythm, as if whole areas of the building were being evacuated. Neither of them move at all. They are left in the last square.

What time is it?

Paul Eight.

Elsa Wow.

Paul I know.

Elsa I must get going.

Paul Yes.

Elsa It's silly. We must be the last people here.

Elsa doesn't move at all, just stays, sitting on the desktop. Paul keeps quite still, waiting to see what will happen.

Paul What about you?

Elsa What?

Paul Victor said you used to go to the meetings.

Elsa I did.

Paul You stopped?

Elsa I did.

Paul You don't . . .

Elsa What?

Paul I'm asking if you're clean.

Elsa Well . . . I have two children, remember?

Paul Does that make it easier?

Elsa Not at all. No, on the contrary.

Paul Then why do you mention it?

Elsa Because whatever feelings of guilt you suffer from, I suffered much worse.

Paul I see.

Elsa Yes, exactly. (*Elsa is looking at him very hard now.*) That's my point. That's what I'm saying. Paul. I'm not a stranger to self-hatred.

Paul No.

> *His name sounds direct, almost challenging from her lips. Elsa shifts slightly.*

Elsa Why do you imagine Victor employed you?

Paul I honestly don't know.

Elsa Why do you think?

Paul I suppose some Medici-like munificence.

Elsa Do you think?

Paul Isn't that the idea?

Elsa You say.

Paul It can hardly be for my copywriting skills. He likes the notion of a poet, in-house. The cyber-monarchs acting as sponsors of the arts . . .

Elsa Is that it?

Paul Commanding the ideas of the day. Intellectual patronage. Something like that.

Elsa Or pity? Do you think pity comes into it?

> *Paul looks, wary.*

Paul You say. You tell me. Why do you think Victor employed me?

Elsa I imagine in some way you remind him of me.

Paul looks her straight in the eye, not responding,
giving nothing away.

Paul Tell me what we're doing. Tell me what's going on.

Elsa slips down off the desk, moving for the first time.
She smiles, apparently at ease.

Elsa What are we doing? We're talking.

Paul Thank God.

Elsa That's all. (*Elsa sits in a nearby chair. She crosses*
her legs.) I've no right to talk about this . . .

Paul Go ahead.

Elsa As you say, I hardly know you. I came in here by
chance. I was looking for Victor actually . . .

Paul He'll be back soon, he said.

Elsa Well, good.

Elsa smiles. They look at each other, neither shifting
their gaze.

Paul You see, it's the bit . . . forgive me, it's the moment
when you rustle your legs . . .

Elsa I'm sorry.

Paul No. The sound of your stockings.

Elsa I'll try to sit more discreetly.

Paul It's fine.

Elsa barely moves.

Elsa Are you going to hold on and wait?

Paul I've nothing else to do. My flat's empty as usual.
And there's nothing in the larder.

Elsa You should stock up. What do you live on?

Paul Pulses, they're called. And cheap nourishing stews.

Elsa is gazing at him, unwavering.

They tell you at the meetings not to get hungry – hunger's the enemy, they say –

Elsa Or angry –

Paul Hungry. Angry. Lonely. Tired.

Elsa Oh no. You mustn't be any of those.

Paul looks down, red, embarrassed.

Paul The point is, you see, it's not just Clem.

Elsa No . . .

Paul I don't mean just Clem I have to avoid. Ridiculous. All women I have to avoid.

Elsa Yes.

Paul I'm happier with blokes. Or in groups. Five's a good number. Or four. Two makes me jumpy. (*Paul looks down again, overwhelmed.*)

Elsa Yes.

Paul Forgive me, speaking generally . . .

Elsa Of course.

Paul In general.

Elsa Of course.

Paul Talking is fine. This is fine. Talking to you is fine. But all contact, any real closeness I have to avoid. I'm a recovering alcoholic. (*Paul checks with her, but she does not react.*) What's good is, I've had to face the question: what makes me drink?

Elsa What was the answer?

Paul Finally: anger. It's anger. Anger makes me drink. Therefore I have to avoid anger. (*Paul checks with her again.*) Another way of putting it. Emotion made me drink.

Elsa So what do you do about that? Avoid emotion?

Paul Yes.

Elsa Avoid life. (*Elsa goes onto the attack, ignoring his protest.*)

Paul No.

Elsa You think it's that simple? H-A-L-T! Hungry! Angry! Lonely! Tired!

Paul No.

Elsa You think it's that easy? You really sit there and buy that stuff, do you?

Paul grins, side-stepping her question.

Paul It's quite convenient actually. Anyone you don't like you can tell them to fuck off. You're licensed. Anyone gets on my nerves I have the perfect reply. 'I'm sorry. You're endangering my recovery.' That's the advantage of it being a disease.

Elsa Is it a disease?

Paul Of course it is. It's an illness.

Elsa That's what they tell you. That's what they want you to believe.

Paul It's not a question of being *told*. You've been to the meetings. I'm not being *brainwashed*! It's not *brainwashing*!

Elsa They love saying that. 'It's a disease and it's incurable.'

Paul So it is.

Elsa It's for life. For the rest of your life you're an unexploded bomb.

Paul looks at her warily.

Is that what Clem thought?

Paul Clem?

Elsa Yes.

Paul I don't know. I don't know what Clem thought.

Elsa She blamed the drink.

Paul Yes, of course.

Elsa That's what I hate. Clem sleeps with twelve men and she blames the drink.

Paul Now look . . .

Elsa She doesn't blame herself.

Paul Well . . .

Elsa You see that's what gets me. Paul, I'm telling you, you have to break out. (*Elsa impulsively gets up, animated now, excited as if a problem were solved.*) Look at you for goodness' sake, you're thirty, you write like a god . . .

Paul Don't say you read poetry as well.

Elsa We read it together.

Paul My God! In bed?

Elsa Inevitably. *This Too Shall Pass.* Sometimes to the children.

Paul Stop.

Elsa Why?

Paul I'm a poet. One reader's an epiphany. Find two and

you hang out the flags.

But Elsa is not deflected.

Elsa Paul, look at yourself objectively.

Paul How?

Elsa See yourself from the outside.

Paul What?

Elsa You're young, you're talented, you're good-looking. Analyse. What exactly is this problem of yours?

Paul (*frowns*) What *is* it?

Elsa Yes!

Paul 'Analyse'! You sound like him.

Elsa Socio-economically you, Paul, belong to the world's most privileged group.

Paul I don't have a fucking penny!

Elsa Paul, you're an elective intellectual who doesn't have to work in the fields.

Paul Now you sound even more like him.

Elsa You enjoy the company of rich women.

Paul Do I?

Elsa You get to listen to rich women rustling their stockings. (*Elsa is now questioning him with real vehemence.*) Paul, please tell me, just what exactly is your problem meant to be?

Paul picks moodily at the arm of his chair.

Paul You don't know. You know nothing of what went on in my life.

Elsa You lost a girl. That's all.

Paul That is not all.

Elsa Isn't it?

Paul I lost the 'girl', as you call her, because of a habit I had, which was that I could not walk past a glass of whisky at fifty yards without wanting to drink it. No. Correction. Without drinking it. And then the rest of the bottle. Drink humiliates you and then it kills you!

Elsa Do you really believe that was the problem?

Paul Believe it? I know it.

Elsa Do you?

Paul I was drunk for ten years!

Elsa just looks at him, unrelenting.

Elsa Paul, not everything that happens is always your fault.

Paul I didn't say it was!

Elsa No, you didn't. But I look at you and I know you. I *was* you, remember? I was twenty-five, an idiot, and coked out of my head. 'I'm not a stranger to self-hatred.' Remember?

Paul I don't know what you're saying!

Elsa Yes you do. That's what's interesting. In your heart you do. (*Elsa is clear, as if she has just understood something.*) Why do you think Clem slept around?

Paul No. You tell me. Why do you think she did?

Elsa Do you really want to know?

Paul Yes.

Elsa It'll come as bad news.

Paul Break the news.

Elsa Really?

Paul I can take it. I promise. Please. I can take it.

Elsa pauses a moment to take aim.

Elsa Clem slept with other men because that was her choice.

Paul No!

Elsa Yes! That's what she chooses to do. You know how I'd put it? That's who she is. That's her identity. She's twelve-man Clem. Grant her the dignity of her own actions. Because when you blame them on your drinking then insidiously you begin to insult her.

Paul No.

Elsa Yes! She's an adult. She's a grown-up. It's her life. She chooses to sleep with twelve men! That is her magnificent choice. (*Elsa has raised her arms above her head. Now she turns back to Paul with the definitive diagnosis.*) Paul, you are not addicted to alcohol. You are addicted to blame.

Paul is shaking his head in protest.

Paul I can't believe this. I can't believe what I'm hearing.

Elsa Why not?

Paul Because I drove this woman . . . I know what I did: I drove this woman from my bed by my behaviour.

Elsa Did you?

Paul By serial dishonesty. I lied.

Elsa My God! Serial, you say?

Paul I told lies consistently for the eighteen months we were together. I barely let out a single word that was true. I deceived her.

Elsa Yes, but why?

Paul Why do you think? Like all drinkers. To hide my drinking, of course.

Elsa Was that all?

Paul No.

Elsa What else did you lie about?

Paul Oh, things.

Elsa What things?

Paul Everything! What does it matter? It becomes an attitude.

Elsa Say.

Paul looks at her, reluctant to go on.

Say.

Paul If I'm honest . . . also to hide my contempt.

Elsa Your contempt?

Paul Yes.

Elsa That's a strong word. Contempt for what, Paul? Hide your contempt for what?

Paul I'm not telling you.

Elsa Why not?

Paul Because it's none of your business. (*Paul hesitates a moment.*) Well if you want to know, I hid my contempt for her acting.

Elsa Why?

Paul Because it was fucking awful.

Elsa I see.

Paul Yes!

Elsa Bad, was it?

Paul It was embarrassing. It was the pits.

Elsa Ah now . . .

Paul Yes!

Elsa Well now . . .

Paul That's what I really thought. She tried to be alluring but she came across as vulgar. And she couldn't say the lines.

Elsa is nodding, at last at the heart of things.

Elsa So. Now we progress. Now we understand. You were in a long-term relationship with what is known technically as a 'bad actress'.

Paul Very funny.

Elsa Seems to me clear what drove you to drink.

Paul You know nothing. You insult me. You know nothing at all.

Now Elsa moves in for the kill.

Elsa And one more thing. Was she clever? Was Clem clever? Was Clem as clever as you are?

Paul looks at her, not answering.

You fell in love with an idea, didn't you, Paul? You had an idea of her.

Paul Yes.

Elsa Oh yes. And one more thing. One more thing, Paul. About her acting. Was its awfulness your fault as well?

There is a silence. Then Paul suddenly gets up and moves a distance away, further than we knew the area reached. Elsa stays where she is.

Paul I can't do this. I can't. I can't do this.

Elsa Do what?

Paul Argue. Relate. (*Paul shakes his head, overwhelmed.*) Honestly, I got out of this. I stopped this. I put it all behind me.

Elsa All what behind you?

Paul This. This sort of thing. (*Paul repeats his mantra of security.*) I've been dry for fifty-six days. I have one hope. I have one thread of hope. I go to the meetings. I go home. I listen to music. I can't . . . (*Paul stops dead, unable to speak.*)

Elsa You can't what, Paul? You can't what?

Paul I can't . . .

Elsa gets up and moves quickly across the room to him. She takes him in her arms, cradling his head. He is crying. Elsa holds him, then she looks into his eyes.

Elsa You can't what?

Paul begins to kiss her. Gently, their mouths together, he pushes her down against the top of a desk. They stay in each other's arms, passionate. Paul begins to pull at her white shirt, unloosening it from her skirt. For a few moments it looks as if they will go on. But then they separate. They move to different parts of the area. After a while Paul speaks.

Paul For you it was easy. It was easy for you. You had Victor. Isn't that right? 'Oh no problem! I kicked alcohol. I didn't need AA.' But you had Victor to help. Who do I have?

Elsa Me. You have me.

Victor returns, carrying a briefcase. The atmosphere is

not suspicious, because Elsa and Paul are some way apart. Victor is oblivious to what has happened.

Victor Paul. (*He smiles.*)

FIVE

Paul moves out of the scene to talk to us. Behind him, the feeling of the stage lightens and changes. Victor and Elsa disappear.

Paul On the whole, all things considered, I think I can say now with some certainty that Elsa was not what I needed. I was a recovering alcoholic. I needed stability. An awful lot of fascinating things happen when you fall in love with Elsa Quinn. But I don't number stability among them.

   Jung says that when we love another person what we are really doing is trying to compensate for a lack in ourselves. But Jung also says that the search to complete yourself with another person can never succeed.

SIX

Summer. Sunshine. A feeling of outdoors. Victor is heading towards Paul. He is more casually dressed than we have seen him before – without a jacket – and he is wearing sunglasses. He is carrying a silver tray with two beautiful glasses on it. He proceeds to set them out with elaborate care on a garden table. Beside them, he lays out nuts and olives.

Victor I'm making margaritas, but there's no way I'm going to offer you one.

Paul There's no way I'm going to drink one.

Victor Quite right.

He sets down the tray. Paul stands looking out at the evening. Victor is skittish, in wonderful spirits.

And suddenly it's summer at last.

Paul Mmm.

Victor Beautiful, isn't it? The Park stretching away . . .

Paul You're very lucky.

Victor smiles at him from the table.

Victor Do you remember how to make them?

Paul Not clearly.

Victor You put the glasses in the fridge. You put the salt round the glasses.

Paul You put the tequila in the freezer.

Victor Yes, and the cointreau in the shaker.

Paul That's right.

Victor Your aim is something lip-puckeringly cold. It should have the kick of a donkey. Cold as hell in the mouth, then hot as hell as it goes down. Is there anything better?

Paul It depends.

Victor flashes a smile at Paul.

Victor Scientists say it's the whole opposition of taste, and so on. That's how taste works. Fire and ice. Salt and sugar. You get the idea.

Paul I do.

Victor Contradiction. At the very heart of life. Wouldn't you say?

Paul I agree.

Victor Contradiction at the heart of everything. Life and death. We're here. Then we're not. It's a dynamic conception of the world. No still, no pause.

Paul Yes.

Victor I'm sure Elsa's coming out. She's somewhere around.

Paul With the children?

Victor Perhaps. (*Victor turns, suddenly distracted.*) Do you know what I hate? When people say, 'The argument generated more heat than light,' they say. I hate that expression. God, I hate it. What a wimpy thing to say! Heat *is* light. They're intimately connected.

Paul Of course.

Victor 'The argument generated heat, and therefore light.' That's what they should say.

Paul People are frightened.

Victor I suppose.

Paul People are frightened of conflict.

Victor People aren't born any more – they're knitted. (*Victor looks a moment at the two glasses.*) I can get you a Diet Coke.

Paul Thank you.

Victor If I'd thought I'd have stocked up with elderflower juice.

Paul I'm fine. I'm used to it.

Victor All those wonderful things you all drink nowadays.

Paul I know.

Victor It's like vegetarians. They don't have to make do with pasta bake any more.

Paul Quite.

Victor Two million people in AA. So the dear old market floods you with over-priced juices. After the pink pound, the dry pound, eh?

Paul Something like that.

Victor They find it irresistible. Never underestimate the illusion of choice. (*Victor smiles at Paul, then gestures expansively at the surroundings.*) So what do you think?

Paul What?

Victor Of the place?

Paul Oh, it's wonderful.

Victor It is, isn't it? We've only been here six months. I don't know if Elsa told you . . . (*Victor stops.*)

Paul What?

Victor I don't know what Elsa's told you. In general.

Paul Oh. In general, she's told me . . . just this and that, really. I've only met her a couple of times, I think.

Victor frowns.

Victor About what?

Paul About?

Victor Yes, what's she told you about?

Paul About the house.

Victor I see.

Paul Setting her heart on it and how there's room for the children.

Victor I don't want to bore you with what you already know.

Paul Please.

Victor Bore you?

Paul No. I mean . . .

Victor seems disturbed by the loop.

Victor Elsa – what? – Elsa – what? – told you, for her it's great because it's so near work. She can walk to work. Excuse me.

With no warning, he suddenly goes out. Paul is under some strain. He speaks to himself.

Paul Jesus Christ.

Paul takes his jacket off. Victor appears at once, bearing a triumphant jug of margaritas.

Victor And how *is* work? How are you getting on?

Paul Oh . . .

Victor I'll be frank. I'm surprised.

Paul Why?

Victor I had you down as a Luddite.

Paul I can't think why.

Victor The stereotype of a poet, I'm afraid.

Paul Ah yes.

Victor And a line in your poetry . . .

Paul Which one?

Victor . . . made me think you would not be cyber-literate. Something about unknowing what we already know . . .

Paul But that's what I'm saying . . .

Victor 'All advances retreats and gains are loss . . .'

Paul But that's the very thing I'm saying. I'm saying we can't go back.

Victor I know. But you sound as if you want to. There's a longing.(*Victor smiles.*) Poets always long to go back. Childhood. Lost love. How would poets get by without them?

Paul The poem says . . . well, the poem says we might *wish* to go back.

Victor Knowing less might be nice.

Paul Exactly. We might wish – what? – to be happy peasants again. But we can't.

Victor (*Victor shrugs.*) I'm still surprised at how you've fitted in. Who'd have thought that Paul Peplow turns out to be Plug-and-Play?

Paul But why else did you appoint me? Unless you thought I could handle it?

Victor Some people can't.

Paul And if I'd failed, would you have sacked me?

Victor smiles.

Victor Paul. With relish.

Elsa comes into the garden. She is wearing slacks and no shoes, caught very much off her guard at home. She clearly doesn't know Paul is going to be there.

Paul Ah . . .

Elsa Paul, goodness. How are you?

Victor I'm sorry. I invited Paul here back for a drink. He was at a loose end. I thought it would be nice.

Elsa It is.

Paul Elsa.

Elsa Paul.

They shake hands, a little stiffly. Victor is pouring two glistening margaritas. Elsa turns back to him.

Elsa Are you going to say hello to the children?

Paul (*alarmed*) Oh God, should *I* have said hello to them?

Elsa You don't have to.

Paul I'm not good with . . . (*Paul gestures to indicate imaginary dwarves.*)

Elsa Nobody's good with . . . (*Elsa makes the same gesture.*) Except other . . . (*Elsa makes it again.*) And sometimes not even them.

Victor I'd rather drink margaritas. How was your day?

Elsa Did you get Paul a Coke?

Paul I'm fine. I'm . . .

Elsa What?

Paul . . . enjoying the evening.

Victor seems oblivious of their complicity. He takes his first draft of his margarita.

Victor Perfection.

Victor takes one across to Elsa, who has sat down.

Paul Victor was just telling me what a pleasure he would take in sacking me.

Elsa I've no doubt.

Victor We have a high turnover. I don't apologise.

Elsa 'You have to be ruthless.' Victor always says, 'Oh you have to be so ruthless in life.'

Victor It's true. You do.

Elsa He always manages to imply somehow that it's a terrific effort.

Victor Well?

Elsa You don't like to say, 'Victor, for you it seems to come quite easily.'

Victor It has to be done. You do it.

Elsa It's almost a pleasure.

Victor I wouldn't go that far.

Elsa Wouldn't you?

They smile together, not perturbed. Paul is watching, trying to interpret their behaviour.

Paul I don't think I could look someone in the eye and sack them.

Victor Couldn't you? Why not? What would stop you? If you needed to do it, what would stop you?

Paul Scruples.

Victor Scruples? Scruples about what? Losing their good opinion? Is that what matters to you? That everyone should think you're a nice person?

Paul No.

Victor What then?

Paul That I should *be* a nice person.

They all three smile.

Victor Ah, very good . . .

Elsa Yes.

Victor . . . but can one be nice in this world?

Paul That's a different question.

Victor Is there such a thing as nice?

Paul There's such a thing as good.

Victor There's a noun, yes. Elsa does good. It's clear. She administers a charity. So by definition my wife does good. The homeless acquire homes. The roofless roofs. A wealthy person is no longer judged by how much they are worth, but by how much they give away. But *is* she good?

Elsa I don't claim to be good. (*Elsa has become very quiet.*) This drink is very strong.

Victor Is it?

Elsa Yes. It's very strong. It's almost pure alcohol.

Victor looks at her a moment, then he goes on as if he hasn't heard her.

Victor I've come to think that the only thing which imprisons us is fear of other people's opinion.

Paul I'm not sure what you mean.

Victor God is dead, so there's nobody upstairs. And inside us . . . well, conscience is a weak thing, don't you think?

Paul I'm not sure.

Victor Conscience doesn't stop us doing anything. So what's the regulator? What's the inhibitor?

Paul I don't know. You tell me.

Victor Peer pressure, is that the word? Free yourself from that and you're free from everything.

Paul In theory.

Victor Everywhere people fight for freedom, but they're frightened of the one freedom that's truly worth having.

There's a moment silence. Elsa is quite still.

Victor That's the freedom from other people's opinion. (*He looks at Elsa a moment.*) Another drink?

Elsa No thank you. Not yet.

Victor Pacing yourself?

Paul is frowning, disturbed by Victor's argument.

Paul That seems a rather privileged point of view, if I may say so.

Victor Please. Say whatever you like.

Elsa Victor? Privileged?

Paul There are other freedoms, aren't there? Rather more important freedoms, I'd have thought.

Victor Such as?

Paul Freedom from slavery. Freedom from ignorance.

Victor Ah yes. But isn't this an argument of category? You're talking about fairness, not freedom. And, as we know, people have long forgotten about fair, now they're only interested in free.

Paul Is that wholly true?

Victor Socialism was the present the British gave

themselves for winning the war. Or so it now seems. (*Victor stands a moment, his mood darkening.*) Maybe we don't feel we deserve presents any more.

> *Paul looks at Elsa, who is sharing her husband's sadness. Then Victor moves to pour another margarita.*

Of course if I'd been cleverer I'd have spotted that earlier. I wouldn't have wasted all those years selling newspapers at the factory gates.

Elsa Were they wasted?

Victor I would have entered this business earlier. Hence: I'd be richer. I'd be freer. I'd have an even bigger house.

Elsa You don't think you're being just a little imperial, my darling?

Victor Just a little, yes. Something in the mood of the evening perhaps. (*Victor stands thoughtful, then turns to Paul.*) Did Elsa tell you how we met?

Paul No.

Elsa Don't.

Paul She hasn't told me anything. Much. Except how you helped her with drink.

Elsa (*amused*) As you can see.

Victor I did meet her in a bar, it's true. She was smashed.

Paul Had you been married before?

Victor No.

Elsa Victor was against it when he was young.

Paul On principle?

Elsa He thought marriage unachievable as an ideal.

Paul Really? Why?

Victor For the obvious reasons. Physiological, mostly.

Elsa This is one of Victor's favourite theories.

Paul waits.

Paul Try me.

Victor It's a problem of evolution. Ask a Darwinist.
I believe fidelity's effectively impossible when you're
young. In my experience, you leave the young alone for
five minutes, at once they fuck each other. (*Victor turns
casually to Paul.*) You'd know about this.

Paul Would I?

Victor I'm speculating.

Paul Is that right?

Victor I look at the young men in my office – I miss
nothing, I love office romance, I adore it – I look at them
all with their stiff little cocks, and the women wet, wet
with longing, longing for adventure and I think: no
chance. The evolutionary imperative. There we are.
(*Victor shrugs at the inevitability of it all.*)

Paul You think to get married you have to be older?

Victor Plainly, it's a plus.

Elsa Say Victor's age.

Victor At my age at least you have a chance.

Paul But Elsa was young.

Victor Yes.

Paul Well?

Victor She was also exceptional. And she had two children.

Paul is taken off guard.

Paul I didn't realise.

Victor Yes.

Paul I thought they were yours.

Victor Not mine. No. We have no children.

Paul I'd misunderstood.

Elsa I arrived with the children.

Paul frowns.

Paul So – what? – you just walked into a bar and saw her?

Victor She was irresistible.

Elsa Tell Paul what you said.

Victor Oh. I told her she was fruit which had fallen to the ground. (*Victor colours at the memory of saying it. At once it's intimate between them.*)

Elsa A long time ago.

Victor Not for me.

Elsa Soft fruit.

Victor stands behind her. She reaches out for his hand. Paul watches.

Victor hates philanderers.

Victor It's true. I do.

Elsa He hates them.

Victor You say to a girl you can't live without her.

You say to her, you're my whole world. Then a few weeks later you say the same thing, with just the same conviction, only this time you're saying it to someone else. So what's your excuse? Were you lying the first time? No, no, people say, 'I believed it at the time.' But that's not good enough. Things are true or they aren't.

Paul frowns.

You don't agree?

Paul More, I don't quite get it.

Victor Why not?

Paul Because you yourself were saying – just now – even just now you were saying things change. Things evolve.

Victor They do.

Paul Life is contradiction, you said.

Victor So it is. That's right.

Paul Well?

Victor looks at him a moment. Then he puts his hand on Elsa's shoulder.

Victor Essential we hold on to something, then, isn't it?

Elsa is quite still. Then Victor lets go of her and heads out.

I'm getting you a Coke.

He's gone. At once Paul moves away.

Paul Jesus Christ.

Elsa What? What's wrong?

Paul (*imitating Victor*) 'Essential we hold on to something, then, isn't it?'

Elsa Oh . . . (*Elsa waves a hand, to imply it means nothing.*)

Paul I'm not going to survive. I can't survive this.

Elsa Why not?

Paul Something's going on.

Elsa It's Victor.

Paul Something I don't understand.

Elsa He's just being Victor, that's all.

Paul Why does he want me to drink? I've been sixty-eight days sober. It's the longest I've ever been sober. And now he wants me to drink. (*Paul turns away, in anguish.*) Jesus, they tell you at the meetings. It's the golden rule. At all costs, avoid stress. Never get yourself into stressful situations.

Elsa Do you want a margarita?

Paul No thank you.

Elsa It might get you through.

Paul No thank you!

Elsa It's getting me through. (*Elsa smiles to herself.*)

Paul What is this? Faust?

Elsa I don't think so.

Paul Is he Mephistopheles? Am I playing Faust? I'm to make a contract, am I? To lure me to my doom?

Elsa I don't think so.

Paul What's the idea? I'm to raise a glass to my lips and be magically transformed into a human being again? (*Paul frowns, disturbed.*) What was it – was it just chance that he asked me back here?

Elsa Of course. Chance.

Paul It doesn't feel like it.

Elsa That's Victor. It's whim.

Paul (*imitating Victor*) 'Stiff little cocks'! What is going on? 'The young men with their stiff little cocks . . .' (*He turns to her.*) Is he weird or what? Is this some kind of set-up?

Elsa No.

Paul Have I fallen among troilists? What are you? Three in a bed?

Elsa Hardly.

Paul I thought that sort of thing only happened in Surbiton.

Elsa It does.

Paul Among bank clerks. Or druids. It doesn't happen in central London. Does it?

Elsa Paul . . .

Paul Let me know if we're all going to bed because three's my unlucky number.

Elsa It's everyone's unlucky number.

Paul I told you the other night: groups are fine. And two is at least natural. But my experience of three is not good.

> *But Elsa is amused, unable to take him seriously, and knowing he doesn't either.*

Elsa Paul, there is no conspiracy. It's a summer evening. Nothing is happening. We're having a drink and enjoying the evening.

> *Paul turns and looks at her.*

Paul He knows, doesn't he?

Elsa Of course not.

Paul He knows what happened.

Elsa How? How would he know?

Paul Because he knows everything!

Again, Elsa just smiles.

Elsa Paul, he's a man.

Paul You think so?

Elsa He's a man like any other.

Paul Not quite. A man with the trickiest conversational style of anyone alive. Talking to him, it's like walking across a minefield in dark glasses.

Elsa You get used to it.

Paul One word wrong and you're dead. I feel like Oedipus on the Somme.

Elsa Faust! Oedipus! What goes on in your head?

But Paul is already shaking his head in indignation.

Paul Elsa, you're married for Christ's sake, and you have two children.

Elsa So?

Paul What the hell did we do? I've been thinking ever since, what the hell were we doing?

Elsa What do you think we were doing?

Paul We're not doing it again.

Elsa We kissed.

Paul Yes.

Elsa We kissed in the office.

Paul Yes. It was great. But we're not doing it again.

Elsa How was it? (*Elsa is smiling, having picked up on what he has said.*) How did you say it was?

Paul I won't even discuss it.

Elsa 'Great', did you say?

Paul No.

Elsa Did you say 'great'?

Paul No.

Elsa What's 'great'? What does 'great' mean?

Paul Don't do this to me.

> *There is a silence. Then Paul moves away again, trapped. It is very quiet and intimate between them.*

All right, I know what you're going to say but I'm not going to listen.

Elsa 'Great' meaning you were touched?

Paul All right . . .

Elsa 'Great' meaning I reached you? Something reached you? Something made you feel you were alive?

Paul Yes. (*Paul is very quiet, as if talking to himself.*) He's coming back. I can tell he's coming back.

Elsa 'Great' meaning you're not sitting alone in a room in Camberwell? 'Great' meaning for ninety minutes in my company you weren't actually scared?

Paul I'm scared now.

Elsa Why?

Paul I'm scared. I can't love you without alcohol. If I'm to love you I have to have alcohol.

Elsa It isn't true.

Paul Alcohol is bound up in love. (*Paul holds up a hand to prevent her answering.*) You know nothing. I don't believe you're alcoholic. I am alcoholic. (*Paul turns to face her.*) Elsa, I can love you and drink. Or I can not love you and not drink. That's the choice.

Elsa Nothing in between?

Paul No.

Elsa Nothing? For the rest of your life?

Paul doesn't answer.

That's the choice for the rest of your life?

Paul I don't have a life. I threw my life away. I left my life behind me on the motorway. I threw it away in a bottle.

Elsa Why?

Paul Because I had no faith.

Elsa In what?

Paul In myself. In the future. I drank because I had no faith.

Elsa And now?

Paul looks at her, straight in the eye.

Paul Stick with Victor. Victor has faith. And I don't.

Before he can speak, Victor comes back in carrying a Diet Coke. He is in even more cheerful spirits.

Victor Diet Coke, so it is.

Paul addresses us directly.

Paul (*to us*) Victor came back . . .

Paul continues the scene.

Well that's been worth waiting for.

Victor Good.

Paul I could murder a Coke.

Victor As they say.

He hands him the Coke. Paul speaks to us meanwhile.

Paul (*to us*) The sun went down over Regent's Park and the three of us sat on the terrace just watching the lovers. The young lovers paraded before us in the sun . . .

Paul continues the scene.

Victor Perhaps you'll have dinner with us.

Elsa Yes.

Paul Thank you. I'm not sure I can.

Victor There's a restaurant round the corner. I was there the other evening.

Elsa I went with you.

Victor That's right.

Elsa We were there together.

Victor That's right. (*Victor stops, disturbed by her interruption.*) Well, that's what I'm saying.

Paul snaps open his can of Coke. Elsa smiles sweetly at him.

Elsa Victor sometimes forgets I exist.

Victor Their menu is delightfully Greek.

Paul Oh yes?

Victor It offers 'steak cooked on your desire'.

Paul Goodness.

Victor I told them: I'd love my steak to be cooked on my desire. In fact, when it comes to it, I think I'd like a whole Mongolian barbecue cooked on my desire. And everyone could feast. Know what I mean? (*Victor beams triumphantly, a touch of extravagance entering his manner.*) The whole world could feast on my desire.

Elsa Are you drunk, Victor?

Victor I am going to enjoy the benefits of another margarita if that's what you're asking. (*Victor pours himself a third drink. He leers a little.*) My third.

Paul Perhaps I should be going.

Elsa You're drunk.

Victor I am free to drink, so I shall.

> *Victor lifts his glass, beaming, expansive. Paul turns again to us.*

Paul (*to us*) We watched the young people moving round the Park, lying on the grass, kissing, easy, the girls resting on the young men's shoulders, the young men resting in the young women's laps. How real their happiness seemed and how simple . . .

> *Victor has moved behind Elsa's chair and put his hand again on her shoulder, the two of them making a picture of happiness. Paul smiles at them, at ease. Evening is coming down. We have jumped time.*

(*to us*) How simple it would be to be happy.

Victor 'Candy is dandy but liquor is quicker.' Paul and I discussed this expression when we first met.

Paul We did.

Victor Do you actually know what it means?

Elsa I think we can guess.

Victor Paul?

Elsa Surely isn't it to do with women . . .

Victor That's right . . .

Elsa How women are seduced?

Victor You can send women gifts, flowers and so on. But finally the most effective procedure is to get them drunk.

There is a silence.

Huh.

Paul turns to address us.

Paul (*to us*) Victor talked on . . .

Paul turns back. We have jumped time again.

Victor I always say the first million dollars is the only million you can make honestly.

Paul Is that right?

Elsa Oh Victor . . .

Victor A million is the most an honest man can make. Anything beyond is crookery, pure crookery . . .

Paul turns to us.

Paul Victor talked. He talked, it seemed, to fill the air, to fill the space between us, so that none of us need be lonely . . .

Paul turns back. Time is now jumping freely.

Victor I prefer jazz to the classics and always will. What about you?

Paul Oh . . .

Victor A jazz musician is someone who never plays the same thing twice. The classics mystify me. Why listen again when they're always the same?

Elsa They deepen.

Victor Do they?

Elsa They deepen each time.

Paul turns to us.

Paul (*to us*) He talked as an act of kindness, as a version of generosity. He talked so that none of us need stop, none of us need ask ourselves what we were feeling . . . (*Paul turns back.*)

Victor I read in the paper: apparently they did a survey. Bus conductors, on average, live five years longer than bus drivers.

Elsa What does that prove?

Victor Up and down the stairs. Up and down, up and down. The activity may be meaningless but the very fact of it keeps you alive.

Victor mimics the movement on the stairs with his hand. Paul turns to us.

Paul (*to us*) Did he talk because he knew, or did he talk because he didn't know? (*Paul turns back.*)

Victor The personal computer, I would have to admit, is the only significant human invention which is exactly half the size of the instruction manual you need to understand it.

Victor laughs, as if the idea satisfied him. Paul turns to us.

Paul (*to us*) Nothing had passed between us save a kiss, one kiss grabbed one evening in an empty office . . .

Victor I often say it's like buying a book where the footnotes are ten times longer than the text.

Elsa Yet people go on buying them.

Victor People!

Paul (*to us*) Why had she given it? What had it meant?

Elsa stretches in her chair, like a cat extending itself.

Victor Another margarita?

Elsa Thank you. I will.

Paul turns back to us.

Paul (*to us*) The mystery of it seemed to deepen as the evening went on. And its promise.

There is a long silence. Time has jumped. It is nearly dark. The last of the sun's rays gleam across the Park. The torrent of talk has come to a halt. The evening turns purple. Elsa speaks very quietly.

Elsa Victor always says we can't know.

After a moment, Paul realises she was talking to him.

Paul I'm sorry. I'm sorry, I wasn't listening. (*Paul turns and stares at her.*) I was miles away.

Elsa Victor says we shall know nothing until we are laid out on our zinc beds.

There is a long silence. The light is unearthly. Victor and Elsa are both looking at him as if he has been asleep. Paul is lost for a reaction.

Paul Goodness. What a macabre thought.

Victor Not really. I'm hoping that afterwards they're

planning to tell me what everything meant, because there seems very little chance of finding out at the time.

Paul You sound as if you're becoming religious.

Victor Religious? God, no. One temptation too many. Too addictive. Life being – as we know – all too easily – a series of patterns, a series of addictions. I'd rather break free of the addictions, thank you. (*He looks a moment into his glass, then turns and speaks directly to Paul.*) She won't give me children.

Paul What?

Victor She refuses to give me children. On the grounds she has children already. It's true. (*He stands, waiting for Paul's reaction.*)

Paul I'm sorry.

Victor It's the point of difference between us.

Paul I see.

Victor It involves an act of faith in the future which, given her past, she is unwilling to make. Is that fair?

Elsa It's fair. I had my children accidentally when I was young and stupid. I've never felt quite ready to have any more.

There's a pause.

There it is.

Victor moves back beside her.

Victor It's true. We don't have too many close friends, do we, Elsa? Friends we can talk to.

Elsa Lots of acquaintances.

Victor Sure.

Paul nods slightly, acknowledging the gift of the

confidence. Victor shifts, uneasy.

The boys, believe me, are wonderful.

Paul How old are they?

Victor Oh . . .

Elsa Fourteen and twelve. By different fathers. (*Elsa looks straight at Paul a moment.*) Yes, I made a real mess. Thinking in that awful young way that I could do anything. I could cope with anything.

Victor Well? And you have.

Elsa says nothing.

A passion like ours, it's interesting. It both feeds you but isolates you also at the same time. Perhaps that's why our friends are so few.

Paul watches, sad for them, not knowing what to say.

Read the First Book of Kings. How did King David's courtiers seek to prolong David's life? By laying a young virgin in his arms.

Paul Really?

Victor Unfortunately, one would have to say, he died soon after.

Paul Exhaustion?

Victor History doesn't disclose.

Elsa No, not exhaustion. He was dying anyway. And I wasn't a virgin.

Elsa smiles. There is a moment's silence.

Victor I was in my forties and past thinking I would ever meet anyone like Elsa.

Victor reaches down to kiss her. There is a moment

*of suspended gentleness. Paul watches, then he turns
to us.*

Paul (*to us*) Something in the way he kissed her, and in
the sadness between them . . .

Victor For me, the treatment has been a total success.

Paul (*to us*) Something in the passion, in the passion
between them which was everything and which was
nothing . . .

Victor Eight years of unlooked-for happiness.

Paul (*to us*) A feeling rose in me, so overwhelming, so
strong, that I sat, powerless, handing my life over, no
longer caring where it went . . .

Paul turns back. Victor is standing quite still, lost.

I'd like a drink.

Victor frowns, surprised.

Victor I'm sorry?

Paul I wonder, could I have a drink?

Victor Are you sure? Do you think . . . (*He looks a
moment to Elsa.*) I mean, I'm not saying . . .

Paul I'll just have the one.

Victor looks again to Elsa.

Elsa He only wants one.

*Victor takes one last, uncertain look to Elsa, who is
sitting quite still, watching from her chair.*

Victor Well . . .

*He pours the last of the jug into a glass and hands it
to Paul, who stands up to take it. Then Victor smiles.
A small onset of energy.*

I need to say goodnight to the children. Then we should eat.

Elsa Yes.

Victor Eat with us, Paul.

Paul smiles in assent.

Let me take these things in.

Victor picks up the tray and takes it out. The night is purple. Elsa has not moved. Nor has Paul. The feeling is extraordinarily intimate between them. Paul has not yet lifted the glass to his lips.

Paul (*to us*) The margarita was warm by now. We had sat too long in the sun. But I felt the liquid enter my blood like desire itself. The liquid swelled out in my bloodstream, filling it with longing, as if what I were drinking were not tequila, not fermented grain, but life, the sensation of life, filling me with feeling till I overflowed. I stood in the garden, fear held for a moment at bay, beginning to feel I could help, beginning to feel I could live.

Elsa smiles.

Elsa I'm glad you're here, Paul.

Paul I'm glad, too.

Paul lifts the glass and begins to drink. The stage darkens.

Act Two

SEVEN

The stage is void again. Paul stands before us. He is now dressed in a light macintosh.

Paul Looking back you could say the summer played straight to my weaknesses. No aphrodisiac, no engine of fantasy was ever more powerful than the one that propelled me through that time of storm and high sun. I spent those days in the grip of a fever: the huge and fatal excitement when you truly believe you can help someone else.

EIGHT

An opening of light. Elsa has opened what appears to be a door and is standing inside. She is wearing a light dressing gown. She looks peaceful and warm. Paul is standing outside, soaked from light summer rain. He grins, a little foolishly. He carries an exhausted bunch of wet flowers, still in their paper. Paul speaks with elaborate care, never slopping or slurring, making a careful effort to be coherent.

Elsa My God!

Paul I know. Can I come in?

She stands aside to let him by.

Elsa You're drunk. Oh fuck, are you drunk!

Paul I'm not. I'm not much. I've been drinking.

Elsa I'm going to get you coffee.

She leads him into the house. She turns on a light, which radiates a warm glow. Paul stands, not taking his coat off.

How long have you been drinking for?

Paul Not much.

Elsa No. That's not the question. How long?

Paul How long? Very short. Maybe two days.

Elsa Two days continuous do you mean, or two days since you . . .?

Paul (*frowns*) Since me?

Elsa No, not since *me*. Since you started!

Paul Since what?

Elsa Paul, for fuck's sake have some coffee and shut up because the kids are asleep and I don't know what on earth you're doing here anyway.

Paul Victor's abroad.

But Elsa has already gone out. He tries to raise his voice to explain.

Victor's gone for silicon . . . input. (*Now he talks to himself.*) Implant. Victor's gone for silicon . . . no. No. Victor's gone for silicon . . . Victor's gone for silicon . . .

Elsa has come back.

He's gone for business.

Elsa I know. You don't need to tell me. (*Elsa busies herself getting china and cups.*)

Paul Do I find you just a little bit ratty?

Elsa No. More a little bit guilty.

78

Paul Why?

Elsa Because we thought you could handle it. Victor and I thought you could handle it.

Paul I'm in AA, for Christ's sake – of course I can't handle it! Of course I can't handle it! (*Paul is indignant at the absurdity of it.*) I've fucked up every significant relationship in my life. I have a physio-fucking-what's-it-chemical relationship to alcohol. I'm sick as a fucking dog. I'm an alchie. What on earth made you think I could handle it?

Elsa I don't know. You seemed so . . .

Paul So what? So what?

Elsa So incredibly charming, I suppose.

Paul Oh – what – and that fooled you, did it?

Elsa smiles.

Elsa Enough. It fooled me enough.

Elsa has stopped and put down the things. Paul is close to her.

I'm getting you coffee.

Paul Thank you.

Neither of them moves.

Look at your skin.

Elsa takes the compliment easily. She just smiles and goes out again.

I imagine your childhood rather bracing. Was it? I see you, a small child running in the snow. Bathing in the Zuidersee, that sort of thing. Your father muscular and naked with a long wooden staff in his hand. A monk's cowl. And a glass of pure, clean aquavit.

Elsa comes back in with milk and sugar.

Elsa Have you ever been to Denmark?

Paul No.

Elsa Well, for a start, the Zuidersee's in Holland.

Paul Holland! Denmark! God, you're a pedant.

Elsa We bathed off the Skagerrak if you want to know.

Paul Stone me, the Skagerrak, eh? Seems there's no end to Danish invention. The pastry.

Elsa is looking at him, unamused.

Elsa What are you talking about? Is this what you're like when you're drunk?

Paul Well . . .

Elsa You said it gave you life . . .

Paul It does.

Elsa Tremendous passion and insight. You didn't say it made you regress thirty years.

Paul AA calls it the inner child.

Elsa Well, strangle it.

Paul AA says we've lost our ability to play.

Elsa moves across to get a bottle of whisky.

Elsa Me, I'm going to have a drink.

Paul Oh great.

Elsa And you're not allowed.

Elsa pours herself a scotch.

Paul I'm back among the funny folk, you know. I've rather missed them.

Elsa Which ones?

Paul The ones with big purple scars on their cheeks and terrible stories. Keep bursting into tears for no reason. And throwing punches. I'm on what we call a slip, did you know?

Elsa Yes.

Paul Don't you think it sounds glamorous? 'I'm on a slip.'

Elsa just looks at him.

Elsa You haven't told me what you're here for.

Paul The advantage of being drunk is you don't always have to be too clear about what exactly you're up to.

Elsa Plainly.

Paul Drink makes your targets a little wider. It's so wonderful not to be purposeful for a while. Let go and let God!

Elsa I went, remember? I know the jargon.

Elsa remains sardonic, not charmed. Paul is digging into the pocket of his mac.

Paul And apart from anything, I didn't tell you, I'm writing again.

Elsa I don't believe you.

Paul True.

Elsa Are you saying you can't write when you're dry?

Paul Poetry pouring out of me . . .

Elsa Is that what you're frightened of? Is that what you've been frightened of?

Paul has got out some scraps of paper which he has

now dropped on the floor. He stoops to pick them up.

Paul Poets are stubborn fuckers. Have to be. There's no danger of dying of encouragement. (*Paul holds out one page, then carefully puts it back in the notebook he has also extracted.*) I wrote a poem about you. It's here somewhere. Oh yes. A few drinks and move over, Wordsworth. (*Paul puts his notebook back and pats his pocket.*) I mean, they don't tell you that, do they? That night with the margarita, I took one sip and I thought, 'Oh yes. I remember. Drink makes you happy.'

Elsa Briefly.

Paul Oh, what, and we look down on 'briefly', do we?

Elsa We distrust 'briefly'. (*Elsa has got up and is pouring herself another scotch.*)

Paul Are you having another one?

Elsa Are you counting?

Paul Cunning, Baffling and Powerful. That's what they say at AA.

Elsa I remember.

Paul They keep saying that alcohol is Cunning, Baffling and Powerful. Again, like it's meant to be bad. But is it? Are those things bad? When they say them, I always think 'Oh it sounds rather nice.'

Elsa shifts, a little uneasy.

Elsa Paul, have you considered? I think it's possible you may be going through a phase.

Paul I can see that.

Elsa Did anyone ever broach the subject of 'denial'?

Paul Denial?

Elsa Yes.

Paul It's such a shitty concept. Don't you think?

Elsa Well . . .

Paul It's so wonderfully convenient. 'I'm feeling better today.' 'Are you? Are you? *Really*? You must be in denial.' (*Paul wanders across the room, expanding.*) I think denial was only invented to bring people down. Just in case they might begin to feel happy. 'Yes I truly feel I'm starting to get over my problems.' 'Poor fucker. Must be a bad case of denial.' I mean, no chance you might actually be getting somewhere, no chance you might actually be achieving something – oh no, just call it denial and push you back down. It's too fucking easy. (*Paul stands, angry and indignant.*) People say, 'You drink to escape your problems.' 'Oh yes?' I mean, you could say that given that I can't solve my problems, escaping them isn't maybe such a bad idea.

Elsa What are your problems?

Paul Legion.

> *There's a silence. Elsa looks at him with sudden warmth.*

Elsa Did someone give you flowers?

Paul No. They're for you. (*Paul has only just remembered them. He hands them over.*)

Elsa Poetry. Flowers.

Paul I'd kiss you but I suspect I smell like a pet shop.

> *Paul says it so gently that the mood is not broken. She takes them silently and goes out.*

Elsa I was expecting you.

Paul Really?

Elsa As soon as Victor left the country.

Paul Ah.

Elsa I thought you'd come dog-trotting across the Park.

She's gone. Paul wanders happily round the room.

Paul He's gone to talk megabytes with honchos in San Jose. He's meeting Americans with enormous capacity in their laptops. He's flying by nerd-bird.

Elsa (*off*) He loves it.

Paul He does. (*Paul smiles affectionately at the thought of Victor.*)

Elsa (*off*) It's all boys, have you noticed?

Paul Of course.

Elsa (*off*) Where's Jill Gates, that's what I want to know?

Paul Doesn't exist. Who ever heard of a propeller-head who turned out to have breasts?

Elsa (*off*) It's going to be men. Again.

Paul Just like the Communist Party. Victor's back in the Party. Beards again, but this time in Armani and all owning gliders.

Elsa has reappeared with flowers in a vase and stands a moment, thoughtful.

Elsa I look at him sometimes and I see him with the stub of a pencil in his hand.

Paul You mean like a school kid?

Elsa Earnest like a school kid. His socks round his ankles and a big frown on his face. He's never changed.

Paul All those men have what they call 'immense personal fortunes'. Does Victor have one of those? Did he have one when you met him?

Elsa What are you asking? Am I a gold digger? Is that what you're asking?

Paul No.

Elsa He had nothing.

Paul Like me.

Elsa turns and looks at him sharply.

You've been his luck.

The flowers look dismal in the vase.

Elsa It was clever of you to find flowers with only twenty-four hours to live.

Paul I know. They see me coming.

Elsa No, this way at least I can throw them out before Victor gets back. (*Elsa smiles at him.*) I won't have to answer his questions.

Paul Has he been asking you questions? What did he say?

Elsa When?

Paul After that evening when we all had a drink . . .

Elsa Oh . . .

Elsa looks evasive but Paul ploughs on.

Paul I didn't get it. I mean, I know I'm an unsophisticated boy from the provinces, but tell me, did I misunderstand?

Elsa What?

Paul I don't know. For a start, that whole thing about

being so frantic for children . . .

Elsa Ah yes.

Paul Well? He brought the subject up. Was Victor Quinn actually pushing his wife into my arms?

Elsa What, was he asking if you could do the job for him?

Paul I mean I'm just wondering . . .

Elsa I didn't get that impression.

Paul looks bewildered at her.

Paul So what does he want? What did he want?

Elsa Oh really! It's simple, isn't it?

Paul Is it?

Elsa Of course.

Paul So?

Elsa It's a *marriage*, isn't it? However wonderful. Finally, it's a marriage, like any other and it's reached a point . . . (*Elsa breaks off, exasperated.*) Don't you write about these things?

Paul Do I?

Elsa Aren't you a *writer*? Or does Peter Pan not get mixed up in this kind of stuff?

Paul is taken aback at this sudden flash of aggression.

Paul Don't you think we have to discuss this?

Elsa Why?

Paul He said you had no friends . . .

Elsa We have very few.

Paul And he seemed to be – I don't know – asking me to help.

Elsa Yes.

Paul Well?

Elsa He was.

Paul He wanted me to help! How? In what way?

Elsa Isn't it clear? (*Elsa looks at him a moment, not giving way.*) Isn't it clear what he was saying? We've reached a deadlock, that's all.

Paul How?

Elsa Between us. It's a deadlock between us. So Victor got wild, you could see, Victor began to get drunk because Victor's beginning to get desperate.

There is a moment's silence.

We've reached a point where we don't know what happens next.

Paul waits. For the first time, Elsa lets go, the feeling pouring out of her.

Paul, I go to work every day, for God's sake, I go to the Foundation, I spend the day in practical ways. A hard day's practical work, raising money – being practical, giving people help. What do you call it? 'Putting something back.' That's what I do. I put something back. Then I walk home, I walk back through the Park . . . (*Elsa looks him in the eye again, firm.*) I've done it for six years, Paul. I've put in six years.

Paul So?

Elsa I keep my eyes down. I work every day. I'm calm. I come home, I talk to the boys.

87

Paul What are you saying?

Elsa looks at him a moment.

Elsa I'm saying, yes, it's only because of Victor that the Foundation exists. But it's only because of Victor that I exist.

Paul I see.

Elsa Yes. I feel real. Because of Victor.

There is a silence.

Paul I understand that.

Elsa If you'd asked me ten years ago with my daffy head full of coke and my twat in the air, if you'd met me and asked me, 'Will you make it to the age of thirty-three? . . . '

Paul What, was this in the Tivoli?

Elsa Oh very good . . .

Paul Thank you.

Elsa A Danish reference successfully located . . .

Paul I was pretty pleased.

Elsa looks at him mercilessly.

Elsa No, not in the Tivoli, you wanker – people don't do drugs in the Tivoli –

Paul Don't they?

Elsa I was meant to be a model . . .

Paul I thought you were an air hostess . . .

Elsa I was. Later. I was in Antwerp and Munich and Barcelona – any city you can think of – I was an international junkie . . .

Paul Really?

Elsa . . . of epic proportions. And if you'd said to me . . . yes, one day, one day you'll marry your father – it's true, you'll marry your very own father – or at least someone just like your father, except fifty times nicer, fifty times kinder – then I would not have believed you.

Paul I see.

Elsa Yes.

There is a slight pause.

I married the man my father should have been.

Paul How was your father?

Elsa A pig. A drunk. Yours?

Paul Pig-ish.

Elsa Yes. (*Again, Elsa is unforgiving.*) Paul, I made myself a promise, I made a decision.

Paul When?

Elsa Some weeks ago. You threw me. It was your fault. You threw me off course.

Paul I did?

Elsa Yes.

Paul That night? When we kissed?

Elsa Then. And I made a decision not to discuss Victor with you. Never to discuss our relationship with you. (*Elsa looks at him a moment.*) Whatever happens.

Paul I'm not asking you to dis him.

Elsa It's not a question of dissing him. It's a question of privacy. It's a question of respect.

Paul is frowning, having trouble getting this.

Paul OK. I'm just asking.

Elsa I know what you're asking.

Paul And?

Elsa And I won't tell you.

Paul What?

Elsa Anything. Least of all about whether we're happy or not. There's a line there and I promise you, I'm not going to cross it.

Paul Right.

There's a slight pause.

Are you?

Elsa What?

Paul Happy?

Elsa Well, what do you think? (*Elsa has gone to pour a third drink.*)

Paul Are you sure you need the glass? Isn't the glass a bit . . .

Elsa What?

Paul Intermediate? Why not just jam the bottle to your lips?

Elsa looks at him a moment, not rising to the joke.

Elsa Paul, I have to tell you, you are not the first person to become obsessed with my husband.

Paul I'm not obsessed with him.

Elsa Aren't you?

Paul No.

Elsa I saw a gay man being interviewed on television. They asked him who his favourite Disney character was. He said, 'Minnie Mouse.' 'Minnie?' they said. 'Minnie? That's a very unusual choice.' 'I know,' he said. 'But, you see, she gets me close to Mickey.'

Paul That's very good.

Elsa Well, that's what I'm saying, Paul.

Paul Fair enough. Am I the gay man?

Elsa You tell me. (*Elsa is suddenly insistent.*) I won't be a channel to Victor. That's not what I'm here for. If you want to ask Victor something, ask Victor. If you want to ask me, ask me.

Paul Good.

There is a short silence.

Here it comes. Can I have a coffee?

Elsa Of course.

Paul No mention of Victor in that question at all.

Elsa smiles and goes out. Paul is left alone.

Victor-free. That was a Victor-free question. You have now entered a Victor-free zone. 'This conversation may be recorded purely for professional purposes to instruct trainees at the No-Mention-of-Victor Institute of North London.'

Elsa comes back in with a cafetiere to find Paul still shambling about in his wet mac.

Elsa Are you talking to yourself?

Paul Yes. I'm afraid so.

Elsa Why?

Paul Because that's what it's come to!

Elsa *Why?*

Paul Why the fuck do you think?

Elsa What is wrong with you? What's your problem?

Paul What do you think, for God's sake?

Elsa I don't know!

Paul is suddenly yelling at her, in pain, the whole frustration of the summer at last coming out.

Paul I was out of work. I'm broke. I'm trying to dry out. I'm sent by the worst newspaper in England to go interview the Marxist maniac of Regent's Park.

Elsa So?

Paul I don't *like* being a drunk. Believe me. I don't *want* to be a drunk. Nobody *wants* to be a drunk.

Elsa Of course not.

Paul I've studied a thousand methods of how not to be a drunk. And I promise you the method least recommended by experts – the one thing experts all really agree on – is: don't use the falling-in-love-with-a rich-man's-wife aversion therapy method. (*Paul turns round and raises his arms to the skies.*) Fuck! That's what's wrong!

Elsa I see.

Paul That's my 'problem', as you call it. (*Again, Paul raises his voice in despair.*) I'm hopelessly in love!

Elsa Ah.

Paul Yes.

There is a sudden silence. Elsa smiles, but Paul

persists, desperate to define what he wants to say.

Elsa You don't make it sound very pleasant. What am I meant to do?

Paul And if one more therapist tells me that I only fall in love with what I can't have and it's because I can't have it, that's why I fall in love with it, then I'll punch the fucking bastard on the nose.

Elsa You loved Clem.

Paul I was fly-half to a rugby team that loved Clem. The therapist's point, exactly.

Elsa is watching him, sobered, compassionate as he flails wildly with his feelings.

Whereas you, you have a husband, who's real, who's solid, who radiates solidness – computers! opinions! suits! –

Elsa I have two children.

Paul Well quite!

Elsa Whom I love.

Paul Two strapping Nordic lads. Two boys, two boys who are upstairs as we speak, lying in their beds, their blond, downy hair flopping on their pillows, smelling of pine, and dreaming of manly pursuits . . .

Elsa I must say, Paul, you are what therapists call dangerously introverted.

Paul You think so?

Elsa You do live in a world of your own.

Paul is overwhelmed. At last he yells out what he has plainly wanted to say all along.

Paul Why don't you give him children, for fuck's sake?

Elsa What? (*Elsa looks at him in disbelief.*)

Paul He's a reasonable fellow. Why not give him some children?

Elsa I'm sorry?

Paul Well, that's what he's saying, for God's sake.

Elsa I know that's what he's saying. (*Elsa is so surprised at this attack that she stands lost for a response.*) I know that's what he's saying!

Paul Well?

Elsa Is that what you came to ask? Is that what you're doing here?

Paul I'm not here to *do* anything. I'm here to *be*. I'm here to be the friend you both said you needed. (*Paul shrugs, as if it were easy.*) It's all he wants. He's in his fifties. Be fair. Give the guy a break.

Elsa Give him a *break*?

Paul Why the hell don't you give him children?

Elsa Why do you think? Have you understood nothing? Do you think I don't want to give this man children?

Paul How do I know?

Elsa Do you think I wouldn't if I could?

Paul *So*?

Elsa gestures to the world outside.

Elsa What do you think it's like, walking across the Park, day after day, walking back across the Park, keeping my eyes on the ground? Another day, doing my duty at work? Who do you think I am?

Elsa waits, but Paul says nothing.

I was human trash.

Paul I know.

Elsa I was on the floor of a bar.

Paul I know. Do you think I don't know?

Elsa My knickers ripped in half, my breath stinking of vomit and waiting to be thrown out with the empties. (*Elsa looks at him, her eyes welling up with tears.*) 'Take my hand,' he said. 'Take my hand.' (*Elsa turns away, overwhelmed.*) And since that day he has been steadfast.

Paul I'm sure.

Elsa Not one day has gone by in which he has not been resolute. In which he has not been loyal.

Paul looks down.

Paul I'm sure.

Elsa He gives me confidence when I have no confidence myself. When, like you, I know I could within seconds be back in that bar, like you, back in that gutter again . . .

There is a silence.

He's strong. We're not. We're alike, you and I. We're the same. (*Elsa is suddenly on the verge of tears.*) That's why I don't give him children. I don't have the confidence.

Paul Elsa.

Elsa I don't have the belief.

Paul is watching her now, taken aback at her sudden vulnerability.

Why do you think I sat on your desk? Ridiculous.

Paul No.

Elsa What am I? Absurd?

Paul No.

Elsa Why do you think I laughed with you? Kissed you?
And the reason I was drawn to you . . . the reason I long
for you . . .

Paul What?

Elsa can't speak.

What?

Elsa When I see us together . . . (*Elsa shakes her head,
overwhelmed.*) I see us.

Paul How?

Elsa We go off to bars and go down together, go down
laughing together, spiralling together . . .

Paul No!

Elsa Yes! That's what I see. (*Impulsively, Elsa moves
towards him.*) Tell me I'm wrong.

Paul Elsa . . .

*Violently, Elsa digs into his pocket. She finds his
notebook, which she throws away onto the floor.*

Paul That's my fucking notebook, for God's sake.

Elsa It's not your notebook I'm after.

*Elsa is suddenly possessed, and so, although he is not
resisting, it's a messy struggle as she reaches again into
the pocket of his macintosh. There's a half-emptied
half-bottle of scotch in it. She takes it out and holds it
out in her hand, yelling at him.*

We're the same. Where do we find life that isn't in a
bottle?

Paul moves towards her.

Paul Give it to me.

Elsa No.

Paul Give it back.

Elsa No. (*Elsa moves away from him but he advances.*)

Paul Elsa . . .

Elsa I won't.

Paul I won't drink it. I'll pour it away.

Elsa No.

Paul I won't drink. Elsa, if I'm with you, I won't drink.

Elsa looks at him, not sure. He has his arm extended towards her.

I promise. I make you that promise. (*Paul looks at a pot plant beside him.*) What's this?

Elsa It's a ficus.

Paul I'll pour it in the ficus.

Elsa The ficus will die.

Paul I'll take that chance.

Elsa stands a moment, wavering now.

I'll pour it in the ficus and I won't drink again.

Elsa hands him the bottle. Paul tosses it unopened aside into the pot plant. She moves quickly and throws herself into his arms. They kiss, passionately. Paul takes her head in his hands and looks into her eyes.

He said you were cured.

Elsa Did he?

Paul Yes. He said, one gin and tonic. You drank one gin and tonic, he said. You played Scrabble, he said.

Elsa looks into his eyes a moment.

Elsa Come here. Come over here.

Elsa pulls him towards a sofa. They are pulling at each other's clothes.

Do I look cured?

Now it is her turn to take Paul's head in her hands and to look into his eyes.

Do I feel cured?

NINE

Paul moves out of the scene to talk to us. Behind him, the feeling of the stage changes again, Elsa disappearing into the dark.

Paul What did I think? What did I think at that moment? That I could be solid in the way Victor was solid? Never. I knew I could never replace him. But I felt the power of her and her warmth. The alcohol drained out of me and her warmth filled me. I vanished into her warmth and was consumed.

Victor appears a long way away, reading a file. He stands, quite still.

The hour that followed was the happiest of my life.

TEN

And now Victor, wearing a new, shinier suit, is advancing towards Paul. His manner is louring,

aggressive as he heads towards Paul at his desk. The
evening sun slants across the offices.

Victor Ah Paul, there you are. I'd begun to think you'd
been avoiding me.

Paul Not at all.

Victor Ah good.

Paul No. (*Paul smiles, not dropping his guard.*) You've
been away.

Victor It's true. I must have drawn the wrong conclusion.

Paul I think you did.

Victor Everyone dies after their last meal but that
doesn't mean they were poisoned.

Paul Quite.

   Victor gives him a chilly smile.

Victor And you've heard of our problems?

Paul We've all read in the paper.

Victor There you are. Capitalism at its most infuriating
and obtuse.

Paul Is it any other way?

Victor First the market overvalues us and now –
capricious, arbitrary – it marks us down.

Paul And neither movement anything to do with you.

Victor *I* don't think so. (*Victor scoffs at the silliness of
it.*) The market correcting its own mistakes, it says. It
swallows us up and then it vomits us out. What are we?
Ping-pong balls.

Paul So it seems.

Victor Our value slashed overnight. And everyone says

it's normal. It's accepted as normal. An economy used to *make* things. Now? A world in which ten people do something and the other ninety speculate. Normal?

Paul No.

Victor We've lost our ability to see life as it is. We need poets more than ever, wouldn't you say?

Paul Surely.

Victor To remind us.

> *There's a silence. Victor sits down at the side of Paul's desk and starts reading a file.*

It's a game, nothing else. Because we lack any wisdom ourselves, we will all pretend that the market is wise. It's a form of camp.

> *Victor has not looked up as he says this. Paul is nervous, turning a box of matches over between his fingers.*

Paul You seem calm.

Victor Say what?

Paul It doesn't seem to get to you.

Victor Or is it just that I'm too arrogant to let it show?

Paul (*smiles*) Perhaps.

> *Paul waits, not knowing what Victor wants. Victor goes on reading.*

Is there something you wanted?

Victor No.

Paul I just wondered . . . in particular.

Victor Only to talk to you.

Paul Ah.

Victor looks up.

Victor Why? Should there be?

Paul No.

Victor No hierarchy in the cyber-business. A cat may look at a king.

Victor starts reading again. Paul waits, lost for the purpose of the visit.

Do you never do any work?

But before Paul can answer, Victor erupts unpredictably.

Of course the market gets to me. Of course it does. Why would it not? I'm in a vile temper.

Paul I see.

Victor That's what I'm saying. The humiliation of being judged by people who know nothing.

Paul I'm sure.

Victor I feel like an African dictator. I leave the country for ten days and I return to find there's been a coup. (*Victor looks humourlessly at Paul.*) Not for myself. Believe me, I'm not upset for myself.

Paul No?

Victor The money I lose is immaterial. If the business goes belly-up I'm still a rich man.

Paul Can it go belly-up?

Victor I have my creature comforts. My house, my wife . . .

Paul Yes.

Victor As you know. As you well know.

This time Victor looks straight into Paul's eyes. Paul is

becoming more nervous.

Paul Your 'immense personal fortune', so-called.

Victor Quite so. But I also have an estimate of myself, an idea of myself.

Paul Justifiably.

Victor Please. I don't need corroboration. I don't need praise.

Paul I don't mean to flatter you.

Victor One thing I've understood. Praise is salt water. Drink it and you become thirsty.

Paul You don't have to tell me.

Victor frowns, not understanding.

I'm a writer.

Victor Ah, yes. Exactly. However. It would still be a defeat. Were FLOTILLA to go down.

Paul I don't understand. Can it go down?

Victor As suddenly as it rose. (*Victor looks at him, cheerless.*) There are no profits after all. Only the promise of profits.

Paul People know that.

Victor Yes.

Paul All Internet businesses are about potential. They're about expectation.

Victor But as in all things, people get tired of waiting. Don't they?

Now he is staring at Paul, who is extremely uncomfortable.

Don't you get tired of waiting, Paul? Does life, then,

come down to waiting?

Paul is lost for a moment. He moves slightly in his seat.

Paul Well . . .

Victor The business itself is unchanged.

Paul Of course.

Victor Tomorrow it may be judged to be prospering. That is the nature of the current dispensation. It's tulip mania. It's epidemic suggestion.

Paul (*smiles*) Yes.

Victor Ping-pong balls dancing on fountains! What is believed to prosper prospers. Nothing is but what is believed. Everything becomes a question of confidence. We don't say confidence trick. We say confidence creation.

Paul is unsure how to react but before he can speak Victor becomes purposeful again.

I apologise if we led you astray the other night.

Paul It's fine.

Victor Back on the taste, isn't that what they say?

Paul Yes.

Victor Back on the brew. You tied one on. No, really. I felt guilty.

Paul No need.

Victor Elsa and I felt guilty. It weighed on my conscience.

There is a moment's pause.

Paul Conscience is a weak thing, you said.

Victor Huh. Have you drunk since?

Paul Have I . . .

Victor Since that evening? Have you drunk again?

Paul No. Not a drop.

Paul is firm. Victor watches.

Victor Tell me, this is academic, I'm just asking, there's not a hint of reproach, but do you lie about your drinking?

Paul Compulsively.

Victor I see.

Paul Like all drinkers.

Victor smiles.

Victor All the time or just occasionally?

Paul It's . . .

Victor Though it doesn't really matter does it?

Paul Not much.

Victor Given what you just said.

Paul Exactly.

Victor That's the beauty of lying. You need only do it once to spread infinite distrust.

Paul says nothing.

Good for you. You're right. It's nobody's business but your own. Drink yourself to death if you so please.

Paul Thank you.

Victor Men fought and died in two world wars for the right of people like us to destroy ourselves.

Paul I wouldn't put it quite like that.

Victor Wouldn't you?

Paul No.

Victor How would you put it? How do you explain the current passion for addiction?

Paul Well . . .

Victor Tell me, Paul, why does it have such allure?

There is a sharp edge to Victor's question which makes Paul hesitate, frightened to answer.

People say lack of faith, don't they?

Paul They do.

Victor But do they know what they mean?

Paul I'm not sure what it means.

Victor Me neither. (*Victor looks at him a moment.*) People say to me, 'Oh you're so lucky because you had faith.' As if having faith were such a wonderful thing. But Stalin had faith. Hitler had faith.

Paul That's right.

Victor Faith in itself isn't so wonderful.

Paul No.

Victor Regardless.

Paul Quite.

Victor Would it be wonderful to believe in the Virgin Birth? I don't think so. Or that the trees speak to you? Wouldn't that just mean you were mad? You'd call it faith, but so what? Faith's not valuable. Not in itself. It's what you have faith in that matters.

Paul is silent, just watching.

Paul Of course.

Paul looks nervous, not knowing what Victor will say next. Victor is bitter now.

Victor I had faith. But then it was stolen from me. I was the victim of a robbery. Like millions of others. History came along and clobbered us on the head. No victim support scheme for us.

Paul No.

Victor Just thrown out into the world and told to get on with it. Given a sharp lesson and told we could have no effect. Do I seem ridiculous to you?

Paul Not at all.

Victor I have felt ridiculous. (*Victor shrugs slightly.*) What does it mean to say that I was angry? For years. 'I was angry.' Why? Because the world was not as I wished it to be. Yes.

Paul Is it for anyone?

Victor That's what it came down to.

Paul Hmm.

Victor Of course, it now seems peculiar. What was it? Arrogance? I used to say to myself even then, as I sat stuffing leaflets into envelopes, denouncing iniquity. 'What is this? What are you doing?'

Paul Yes.

Victor I used to ask myself . . .

Paul I'm sure.

Victor Even at the time. Giving my young life. I used to wonder: 'Things are not as they should be, you say? So the purpose of the world is what? That Victor Quinn should be pleased with how it is arranged?'

Paul It's a good question.

Victor 'Who is Victor Quinn? God?'

Paul Hardly.

Victor 'All this rage, all this indignation, what does it mean? What, you feel the world is somehow not meeting your expectation? The obligation of the world being to please Victor Quinn?' (*Victor shakes his head.*) Did I waste those years? Or they did waste me? Or were those the only years I ever lived? (*Victor laughs scornfully at himself.*) Yes, ridiculous. And yet the fire is still in my bones. (*Victor looks suddenly at Paul.*) What do you make of that?

Paul I don't know what to make of it.

Victor Nor me. But am I alone? No. All round me I see this. The means of channelling our anger has gone. We no longer dispose of it. But the impetus of the anger remains. (*Victor suddenly lets go.*) What bloody right do these people have to value us?

Paul None.

Victor None!

Paul However.

Victor looks at Paul.

Victor I took a shine to you, Paul.

Paul Yes.

Victor I took you on because I liked you.

There is a silence.

But you think that I must live with it, is that what you think?

Victor holds his gaze, not relenting. Paul doesn't answer.

The poet! The philosopher! Bringing the message the philosopher always brings.

There is a moment's silence.

Paul You must live with your anger as I must live with my disease.

Elsa has appeared at the back of the area. She is windblown, distraught, as if she has not slept.

Elsa My God, I'm sorry . . .

Paul Elsa . . .

Elsa I was worried.

Paul Are you all right?

Elsa Victor, you're here.

Victor Yes.

Elsa You weren't at home. I tried to call you.

Victor Did you? Nobody told me.

Elsa I've been trying to find you.

Paul has got up awkwardly to greet her, alarmed by her appearance, but Victor has not moved. Elsa approaches them.

I came home and you weren't there.

Victor I'm often not there. I'm here.

Elsa I know.

Victor What, and you were concerned? Why were you concerned, my darling?

Victor holds out a hand towards her. She doesn't take it.

Victor smiles easily at Paul.

As you can tell, we had a row.

Paul I'm sorry.

Victor Last night.

Elsa Yes.

Victor We had a splendid row. It's rare. We never row. I stormed into the night. I did a runner.

Elsa Victor, we're meant to be going to a concert.

Victor Of course. (*Victor frowns.*) When?

Elsa Now.

Victor Would Mozart match your mood right now? I'm not sure he would match mine. All that life-affirming can seem awfully jangly when it hits you at the wrong angle.

Elsa I don't mind.

> *Paul watches as Elsa looks slightly desperately at Victor.*

What are you saying? You don't want to go?

> *Victor looks at her coolly.*

Victor Go with Paul. Take Paul. Affirm life with Paul.

Paul I can't. (*He hesitates a second.*) I have to go to the meeting.

> *There is a long silence. Victor smiles as if he had known this would be Paul's answer. The three of them are suspended. The lemony light fades a little.*

Victor Summer's end, you see. Always a moment of calm. The slight change in the air. Oh, it's still August. The sun beats down. But touched with the knowledge of what is to come.

Paul and Elsa watch him, unsure what he means. The light darkens as he speaks.

Elsa Victor . . .

Victor I met her in a bar, she in a T-shirt, me in a suit. She insulted me for three hours on end, then fell insensible to the floor. You remember? A spirit in her burning like life itself, burning with misdirected passion against itself. Danish, I thought. Interesting. (*Victor smiles, at ease.*) Oh they were fine times together, travelling together, like in your poem . . .

Paul Which one?

Victor The first one we read. 'Travelling to Greece'.

Paul Ah.

Victor That phrase. 'The bougainvillaea thrown like paint against the wall.'

Paul Oh yes.

Victor Very good, that. Well done. (*Victor is lost for a moment in thought.*) We lay on the beach, the sun burning the drugs out of her, at exactly this time of year, her two little boys tied round our ankles like tin cans, clattering like cans wherever we went . . . (*Victor is silent.*) One believed in the future.

Elsa You still do.

Victor Of a kind. Of a different kind.

Elsa is standing behind him, not moving and he does not turn to look at her.

Believe me, I am no less enchanted, no less enraptured with my wife than on the first day I met her. The fascination. In that respect nothing changes. But life changes around you. You realise only later. 'How happy we were.' How much cleverer it would be to know at the time.

Elsa shifts, impatient.

Elsa This is all to do with work.

Victor You think so?

Elsa Of course. You're depressed because of work.

Victor turns and looks at Paul, his face blank.

Victor When the party is over, I pride myself I will know when to leave. Why hang on? I don't want the host yawning all over and longing to go to bed. (*Victor is thoughtful again.*) I read the other day: most people die in the small hours, when their resistance is lowest.

There is a short silence. Then impulsively Victor gets up.

I'm going to get a drink.

Elsa Are you sure that's fair?

Victor Why not?

Elsa In front of Paul.

Paul I've made a new vow.

Victor Have you?

There is a silence. But Victor just turns, quiet, to Paul.

And will this one last?

Elsa Victor . . .

Paul I don't know.

Victor Or will it go the way of all the others? Won't it go down just as the others went down?

Paul Who can say?

Victor Aren't we patterned? Aren't we programmed?

Paul You tell me.

Victor Don't we always promise, 'Tomorrow I'll stop. Tomorrow I'll be good'?

There is a moment's silence. Paul seems nervous.

It's the disease of more, isn't that what they say?

Paul I'm trying to break my pattern.

Victor Good.

Victor looks at him a moment, then gets up and goes out abruptly, in silence. Paul goes to his desk and starts quickly gathering his stuff together. Elsa watches, panicked.

Elsa What are you doing?

Paul I'm going. I'm leaving my job and I'm going.

Elsa Paul . . .

Paul I have to. I have to get out.

Elsa Why?

Paul stops for a moment and looks at Elsa, as if the answer were obvious. Then resumes packing.

Paul It's not hard to say, is it? It's not hard to see why. (*Paul gestures in Victor's direction.*) Look at him, for God's sake.

Elsa Oh really!

Paul Just look at him. Look at his mood.

Elsa So?

Paul What do you think it's about?

Elsa I know what it's about.

Paul Well?

Elsa suddenly raises her voice.

Elsa It's not do with you! His share price is falling!

Paul stands a moment, accusing her.

Paul Last night you quarrelled. You think that's coincidence? You think that's just chance?

Then Paul resumes, frantically throwing his possessions together. Elsa is serious now.

Elsa What are you saying?

Paul It's not love.

Elsa Isn't it?

Paul No.

Elsa I thought it was love.

Paul No. It's addiction. We're addicted to trouble. We both love trouble. And he knows it. He knows what's happening. He knows. It's clear as day. (*He has pointed away into the distance towards Victor. Now he looks at Elsa.*) He knows and he's too proud to say.

Elsa moves towards him, lowering her voice for fear of Victor's return.

Elsa Paul, I was happy with you.

Paul I know.

Elsa For those hours, I was happy with you.

Paul Elsa. I'm happy drinking. So?

Elsa No!

Paul Yes! I'm happy with a drink in my hand. Tell me: what's the difference?

Elsa is shaking her head.

Elsa What do you think? You think I want affairs?

Paul No.

Elsa You think I live that kind of life?

Paul No.

Elsa Is that how you see me?

Paul looks up at her, the answer self-evident.

Then don't run out on me.

Paul Elsa . . . (*Paul shakes his head, helpless now, as if he could do nothing.*)

Elsa You haven't thought. You haven't thought what you're doing. This is who you are. This is you, Paul. You're the person who runs. You think it's to do with alcohol? It's not. Don't you see? It's to do with who you are. Given the slightest reason. Given the slightest excuse. (*Elsa looks at him, pleading.*) You have a friend in trouble. His business is in trouble. You're the first friend he's made in years.

Paul Am I?

Elsa Don't run.

Paul resumes his packing, unconvinced.

Paul You barely know me, Elsa. You barely had time to know me.

Elsa You're scared. You're just scared.

Paul stops, because it's true.

You're scared because you're in love. You're more in love than ever.

There is a silence, and an admission in the silence.

Paul Yes.

Elsa And?

Paul looks tempted for a moment.

So?

Paul You're married, Elsa. You'll never leave him.

Elsa Paul . . .

Paul Yes, I wanted to help. But how do you help a man by sleeping with his wife?

Elsa just looks at him, not daring to move now.

I was trying to help. I thought at last there's something I can do. Something important. Something worthwhile. The miracle of finding two people I like and of them liking me. Two people who've frozen up and who need to thaw out . . .

Elsa stands there, fighting back tears.

I saw the pain you were in and I wanted to help.

Elsa What makes you so stubborn? What makes you so sure?

Paul I am sure.

Elsa Oh it's easy to be you. It's so easy.

Paul Is it?

Elsa Oh yes. The heartbreaker. When anyone needs you, you run. When anyone loves you, you go.

Paul's gaze is steady on her from across the room.

Paul I love you. It's true. Explain. How does it help if I stay?

They stand, looking at each other. Victor comes in, whisky bottle in hand. His mood has darkened.

Victor Not even dusk and there's no one to be seen.

Paul No one.

Victor My modernist corridors deserted.

Paul I know.

Victor Like an architect's model. Glass reflecting only glass. It's a business for obsessives they say. But where are they? On their August beaches, or in their back gardens. Fled. All fled. (*Victor turns with a note of drama.*) And not a soul remains.

It is darkening considerably now.

Whisky?

Paul No thank you.

Elsa No.

Victor pours his own, a large one.

Victor The captain could leave and the ship would sail on regardless. Crew-less. Riding a great wave of purposeless energy. The heaving tide of technology bearing us aloft.

Victor turns and raises his arms above his head, glass in hand. As he does so, by chance, there is the first roar of thunder from outside the windows.

Ah, here it comes. Bang on cue. (*Victor smiles, satisfied.*) No, Victor Quinn is not God, but on the other hand you must admit he has remarkable timing.

Paul I must say.

Victor I timed it.

Paul Is timing one of God's gifts?

Victor Let's say: He heightens His effects.

A flash of lightning and another growl of thunder. Victor grins, happy. He seems not to notice that Elsa has walked away, her arms folded, fighting back her feelings.

Isn't this all we want? The illusion of control. We point – and the lightning flashes. We turn – and the thunder sounds.

The thunder sounds again.

Actions have consequences, we say. But we say it with hope, not with conviction. Because everywhere we see disparity and injustice. Virtue not rewarded and vice not condemned. Only a tangle of intentions – our own fitful intentions . . .

Victor becomes thoughtful, sitting now, staring into his drink. Elsa, growing more uneasy, is about to speak but Victor interrupts.

Elsa Victor . . .

Victor Hmm. I'm pretending not to see. I'm pretending not to notice.

Paul Ah.

Victor I'm drinking my whisky, and ignoring your own intentions. But if I am not mistaken you seem to be clearing out your desk.

Paul Indeed.

Victor An air of drama obtains.

The two of them are looking at each other.

Paul Forgive me. I've made a mistake.

Elsa Paul wants to leave.

Victor I see.

Elsa He's insisting he leaves.

Now it is dark, as before rain. Paul is nervous,

screwing himself up for the task.

Paul Look, the problem is, Victor, let's be honest. I'm actually hopeless at the job.

Victor Really?

Paul You must have noticed.

Victor Again, let's say, I didn't want it to be true.

Paul 'The unsinkable FLOTILLA.'

Victor Huh.

Paul 'Float into the future with FLOTILLA'. 'Hey there, killer, try FLOTILLA.' I can't do it. I can't write to order.

Victor Too much the poet? Too much your own man? (*Victor's gaze does not shift.*) A bad appointment, then. We'll move you elsewhere.

Paul I don't think so.

Victor Why not? Tell me why not.

Paul doesn't answer.

Don't you need money?

Paul Desperately.

Victor Consider it charity.

Paul I couldn't.

Victor Call it a consultancy. Isn't that the rage? Isn't that the dodge? Consultant? All the benefits of a job without actually having to do it?

Paul smiles at the absurdity of it.

You think it wouldn't work? The wrong ethical basis for a relationship, you think?

Victor looks at him, heavy with irony. Paul moves a little towards him.

Paul You've been kind. You've been good to me, Victor.

Victor Thank you.

Paul Nobody ever tried to help me as you have. But I wasn't ready.

Victor No?

There is a silence. Paul glances at Elsa who is watching all the time.

Paul It's my fault. I shouldn't have taken the job.

The thunder growls once more. Victor gets up and pours himself a second scotch.

Victor It's not easy, is it? It's never easy, is it, when you try to help? (*Victor stands a moment, thoughtful.*) I tell you, I was sleeping last night in Regent's Park . . .

Paul I'm sorry?

Victor Didn't I say? I slept the night in Regents Park.

Paul You didn't say, no.

Victor Beneath the stars.

Paul Is that legal?

Victor It's not illegal.

Elsa I didn't know. (*Elsa is standing some way away, shocked.*) I didn't know where you were.

Victor After all, I had to sleep somewhere. Isn't that what men do? When they quarrel with their wives? I slept on some humus, is that the word? A night on the humus.

Elsa I had no idea.

Victor Didn't you?

Paul What about? What was the subject of the quarrel?

Victor Oh, Paul. Are you sure you want to know?

There is a brief silence. Victor looks across to Elsa.

I lay last night beneath the stars, the stars bright above me, felt the earth moving below me, the planet hurtling through space. What does nature care? Not much, I'd say. From the evidence of a night in the Park. But your mind at least opens, and your heart sings. The sounds from the zoo carry on the air.

Victor looks down. Elsa is stone cold.

I lay in the night, listening to the random noises of the night, thinking of Elsa in her bed two hundred yards away. I thought of the many nights we had passed, she shaking from the agony of addiction, the passage from high to low, from frenzy and finally to calm . . .

There is a silence.

Time goes by. It's tough. Life becomes a narrowing. (*Victor turns a moment and looks at Paul.*) Don't we most of all resent the person who helps?

Elsa That's not what I said. That's not what I was saying.

Paul looks between them, unable to fathom the depth of their feeling.

Paul I'll have to go. I'll have to go to my meeting.

Paul moves to the desk to try to take his last things, but Victor is already speaking.

Victor Yes, last night we quarrelled.

Elsa Yes.

Victor Yes, we quarrelled as we have never done in our lives.

Elsa It's true.

Victor As if a whole life's anger rose up and seized us by the throat. (*Victor smiles, gleaming.*)

Elsa He asked me not to drink.

Victor That's it.

Elsa He said I was drinking too much.

Victor looks down.

I defended myself.

Victor She did. She defended herself well.

Elsa That's why we fought. That was the beginning of the fight.

Victor Absolutely. The fight spread, as it were, from there.

Paul Fight?

Victor Argument, Paul. Dispute.

Paul And how was it resolved?

There is a silence. The stage is darkening. Victor turns to look out onto the weather. Then Elsa speaks, clear, compassionate.

Elsa Are we ever cured?

There is a short silence.

Victor Hmm. That's the question.

Elsa How do we know? As well ask: how can you be reborn? Yes I can sometimes go without drinking. Months go by. And, yes, at another time, I taste just one drink. 'Just the one,' I say. Paul is right. It's for life.

Victor is sitting quite still, listening.

Victor says I indulge the children, spoil the children.

Victor You do.

Elsa What else can I do?

Victor You spoil them.

Elsa How can I not? (*Elsa shakes her head.*) Everywhere I go, I see parents who once would have thought it their business to teach their children, to instruct their children. To be placed above their children. Now they drop to their knees, they fall to the floor, they search their own offspring, as if looking for something which they themselves lack . . .

Victor It's true.

Elsa I watch them . . .

Victor Yes.

Elsa Scanning their own children for help.

It is almost dark now, the dark before rain. The three of them are still.

As if life were not a gaining of knowledge, but a loss.

There is a moment's silence.

I was lucky to meet a man. I met a good man. But I met him nonetheless, loved him nonetheless, or rather, have tried to love him. I still do. I still will.

Elsa stands behind him, and now leans down to kiss him. Victor is moved. It comes on to rain outside the windows.

Victor My love.

Victor takes her hand in reconciliation. There is a pause. Then he smiles, gentle.

If God had not intended us to drink, he would not have invented the Sidecar.

Paul (*smiles*) God, eh?

Victor Nor the Silver Bullet. Nor the Silver Stallion.

Paul The Silver Streak.

Victor Exactly. The Dodge Special. The frozen Daiquiri.

Paul Cameron's Kick.

They smile together. The thunder sounds, more distant now.

Victor If we do not enjoy what is attractive we do not feel we are living. Submit to its attraction and we soon lose our way.

Elsa The Moonraker.

Victor The Manhattan.

Elsa The Moulin Rouge.

Victor smiles and sips his drink.

Victor 'Moderation in all things,' said my mum. And died at the age of forty. I miss her. I still miss her. What will they say of me? 'He was a communist, then he made some money. He met a woman. Later, he died. He went from believing people could do everything for each other to wondering whether they could do anything. In his youth people held meetings to organise structures of change. Later they met to stop each other drinking.' In each case, a certain chaos of good-will was apparent. In each case, people reeled away, fearful they had not lived.

Victor is deep in thought. Paul shifts.

Paul I must go.

But before Paul can move, Victor takes firm hold of Elsa's hand, and squeezes it.

Victor It's been a summer, eh? What a summer.

Paul Yes.

Victor It's what a summer should be.

Paul You think?

Victor In the cold months we have to work, we have to live, we have to get on with living. So let us use the warm months for stopping to think. What do you say, Paul?

Paul I agree.

Paul goes to collect his things from his desk. Victor seems restored to life.

Victor So. You're determined to go?

Paul I am.

Victor You submit your resignation?

Paul I do.

Victor It's done. It's accepted. Why not?

Paul Thank you.

Victor Collect your cards. (*Victor smiles.*) It's a freelance culture, that's what they tell me.

Paul That's what I've heard.

Victor The idea of long-term employment is a thing of the past. A job is no longer for life.

Paul Well, I've only been here two months.

Victor Excellent. You have grasped the principle exactly.

Paul Thank you.

Victor has got up to congratulate him.

Victor Paul, you are the modern man. You embody the ideal. Experience becomes a ceaseless search for experience.

Paul Precisely.

Victor Slap! It goes on your CV. 'I worked for Victor Quinn.' (*Victor laughs. He is in good humour again.*) It now seems incredible: my father had a job, and the expectation of the same job for life. Now we live longer, we expect to live many lives, not one. Freelance culture persuades us to believe we may start again. But is it true?

Paul Who knows?

Victor It's a good question.

Paul Indeed.

Victor rubs his hands together, skittish.

Victor Still, everything's fine, as long as we don't sit on the pity pot, as they say at AA. (*Victor smiles across the room at Paul.*) You're not sitting on the pity pot, are you, Paul?

Paul I'm trying not to.

Victor Good. Good for you.

Paul I'm trying to sit anywhere but.

Victor gleams with pleasure at this.

Victor Very good. A very good line.

Paul Thank you.

Victor 'I'm trying to sit anywhere but.' Have you noticed? Everyone always claims that the basis of the English sentence is the iambic pentameter.

Paul Do they?

Victor But it isn't quite true, is it?

Paul Not in my experience.

Victor 'I'm trying to sit anywhere but.' In fact, research shows that the English speak 53 per cent strong beats, 47 per cent weak beats.

Paul Is that right?

Victor It is. (*Victor smiles, pleased.*) In an ideal world, of course, it would be fifty-fifty.

Paul Of course.

Victor Paul.

Paul now has all his things and is standing by his desk, ready to leave.

I never told you this: I once met a man who said he could only become aroused if he'd entered a woman's bedroom by climbing through the window, preferably at a dangerous height from the ground.

Paul (*frowns*) What's that got to do with it?

Victor The higher the window, the better the fuck. (*Victor shrugs, pleased at the thought.*) I'm just saying. I mean, I'm just saying. Nobody's predictable.

Paul No.

Victor We're all different, aren't we?

Paul You could say.

Victor And thank God for it.

It has stopped raining. The evening is lightening outside. Victor is standing opposite Paul. He reaches out and embraces him.

Paul.

Victor holds Paul a moment, his arms clasped around him, then steps back.

Don't fear for me.

Paul I shan't.

Victor Is perfect friendship always brief? History threw me up. It may now cast me down.

Paul I hope not.

Victor Today, chicken. Tomorrow, feathers. It worries me not at all. I have written my epitaph. 'He may have buckled but he did not break.'

The two men smile, uncertain how to part.

And it's time to say goodbye.

Paul Yes.

Victor Not the last time we shall see you, I hope.

Paul No.

Victor You are welcome. You will always be welcome in our home, as you know.

Paul Thank you.

Victor hesitates a moment.

Victor And you must say goodbye to Elsa as well. I insist. I insist. (*Victor turns to her, a little nervous.*) Elsa. If we hurry . . .

Elsa Of course.

Victor At least the second half of the concert.

Victor walks quickly away. He becomes a small figure as his back disappears down the long corridor. Elsa has got up.

Elsa You won't forget me?

Paul No.

Elsa Promise you won't forget me. (*Elsa moves towards him and kisses him on the cheek.*) It's rare, isn't it? It's rare to find love.

*Paul looks at her a moment. Elsa turns and goes
quickly out. Paul puts his things down, and stands.
Then Paul turns also.*

ELEVEN

*The stage clears, and becomes a void again. Paul moves
forward and begins to speak directly to us.*

Paul When you drink again, it's worse. When you
resume, it's worse. And at one level, I know people
believe that when you drink, you're more spontaneous,
you're more 'authentic' . . . but it's hard to be authentic
when you can't get off the bathroom floor.

As everyone knows, Victor Quinn died soon after in a
car crash, poetically not on the M4, but in Leytonstone,
an East London suburb. His blood was three times over
the permitted alcohol level. Elsa went to identify the
body. At last, she said, Victor lay on his zinc bed.

The FLOTILLA software was bought out by Microsoft,
as everything is eventually. After a while Microsoft said
the software was unreliable and replaced it with
products of their own. One day – like the Roman Empire
– Microsoft will itself be replaced. This too shall pass.

I thought of Jung when Victor died. When we love
another person the temptation is to love only what we
lack in ourselves. But the search to complete ourselves
with another person can never succeed.

TWELVE

*Now from the distance, Victor approaches, in characteristic
good spirits, full of life, talking as he comes.*

Victor 'Many are the stories with interesting beginnings, but harder to find are the stories which end well.'

Paul is waiting as if they were meeting for the very first time. Victor smiles and shakes hands with Paul, as he once did, introducing himself.

Victor Quinn.

Paul Paul Peplow.

Victor Of course. (*Victor stands, impressed at meeting Paul.*) That's why personally I prefer to read thrillers. For years I read only thrillers. In a thriller the writer is obligated at least to make an effort at an ending.

Paul That's right.

Victor The novel, to the contrary, remains unresolved.

Seemingly in response to his words, a City church bell at once tolls, deep. The stage changes shape to find Elsa sitting, as she once sat, on Paul's desk.

Paul Elsa crossed and uncrossed her legs, and the bell of a City church rang as she looked at me, not speaking. Just looked at me, looked deep into me.

Elsa looks tenderly at Paul.

Elsa Paul, you are not addicted to alcohol. You are addicted to blame.

There is a silence. Then the lighting changes once more.

Victor When the party is over, I pride myself I will know when to leave. Why hang on? I don't want the host yawning all over and longing to go to bed. I read the other day: most people die in the small hours, when their resistance is lowest.

There is a silence. Then Paul speaks directly to us.

Paul When I think of Victor now it is as a helpless giant, lolling, struggling, tied down with little strings, flailing, now he is dead, in something like innocence . . .

Paul stays facing us at the front of the stage while Victor speaks behind him with his usual crispness.

Victor I prefer jazz to the classics and always will. What about you?

Paul Oh . . .

Victor A jazz musician is someone who never plays the same thing twice. The classics mystify me. Why listen again when they're always the same?

Elsa appears at the back of the stage, miles, miles away from us in a little pool of light.

Elsa They deepen.

Victor Do they? (*Victor turns and begins to walk away from us towards her.*)

Elsa They deepen each time.

Victor reaches Elsa and in a gesture of instinctive love she reaches out and takes him in her arms, embracing him. They are tiny figures in the distance.

Paul The control which Victor always said he was unable to exert, he was indeed finally unable to exert.

The light is fading on Victor and Elsa. Paul pauses. He looks at us a moment.

Myself, I'm sorry. I have to go to a meeting.

Act 1

<u>Sc1</u>   Rd. <u>Paul</u> – memory ...first time ...oh
...Elsa–...

<u>Sc2</u>   Paul & Victor <u>introductions</u> we discover
who they are why they are here

<u>Sc3</u>   ~~Paul~~ – memory – job

<u>Sc 4</u>   <u>Paul & Elsa</u>   More background/flirt etc
kiss – no!   Victor returns

<u>Sc 5</u>   Paul – memory – Elsa – oh dear

<u>Sc 6</u>   <u>Paul / Elsa / Victor</u> – relationships will all
3 together, drink, chat
He sees them / lovers / no ingress
            <u>links</u>
     – ends with his first step back
            towards destruction

Act 2

Act 2   I 4, A

Sc 7   Paul — memory — fever! summer —   ?   I

Sc 8   Paul & Elsa   he is drunk — he has been
          drinking for some time. She stays away ?
          He breaks down, admits, they are together

Sc 9   Paul memory — happiness!

Sc 10   Paul + Victor — tension! His company is ↓
          Hear Elsa they had — fight — chat — fall away
          Paul & Elsa heart to heart — I'm jealous! love! yes!
          Hear Victor — chat   Goodbyes

Sc 11   Paul — memory — end of story — Video compiled

Sc 12   Victor, Paul & Elsa — fragments of memory
          Victor & Elsa off together
          Paul → meeting

Act I

1   P

2   P + V

3   P

4   P + E

5   P

6   P + V + E   some stopping at

Act II

7   P

8   P + E

9   P

10   P + V + E

11   P

12   P + V + E